The Child Care Director's Complete Guide

Other Redleaf Press Books by Christine A. Schmidt

Great Afterschool Programs and Spaces That Wow!

The
Child Care
Director's
Complete
Guide

Christine A. Schmidt

Redleaf Press®
www.redleafpress.org
800-423-8309

Published by Redleaf Press
10 Yorkton Court
St. Paul, MN 55117
www.redleafpress.org

First edition 2017
Cover design by Jim Handrigan
Interior design by Percolator Graphic Design
Typeset in Tiempos Text and Balto
Printed in the United States of America
24 23 22 21 20 19 18 17   1 2 3 4 5 6 7 8

Library of Congress Cataloging-in-Publication Data
Names: Schmidt, Christine A., author.
Title: The child care director's complete guide : what you need to manage and
     lead / Christine A Schmidt.
Description: First Edition. | St. Paul, MN : Redleaf Press, 2017. | Includes
     bibliographical references.
Identifiers: LCCN 2016046503 (print) | LCCN 2017014670 (ebook) | ISBN
     9781605544939 (e-book) | ISBN 9781605544922 (paperback : alk. paper)
Subjects: LCSH: Child care services--Management. | BISAC: EDUCATION /
     Preschool & Kindergarten. | EDUCATION / Leadership. | EDUCATION /
     Reference. | EDUCATION / Administration / General.
Classification: LCC HQ778.5 (ebook) | LCC HQ778.5 .S36 2017 (print) | DDC
     362.7068/4--dc23
LC record available at https://lccn.loc.gov/2016046503

Printed on acid-free paper

To G. Z., my mom, who drove me to be a writer while I drove her crazy.

Management is nothing more than motivating other people.

Lee Iacocca, *Iacocca: An Autobiography*

Contents

Acknowledgments

To my lifelong friend and husband, Rick: thank you for always believing in me, encouraging me when times were hard, and bringing laughter and love into my life. It is only with your understanding, meal service, writing getaways, and constant support and encouragement that this book has become a reality. To my children and grandchildren, who are constant reminders of the positive effect of high-quality learning environments: thank you for constantly reminding me of the uniqueness and vast potential of each individual.

Many thanks go to all the directors, administrators, and professionals across the United States who took time from their busy schedules to discuss their challenges and successes in child- and youth-serving organizations. Their belief in the project and their willingness to help others provided many tips to the new and seasoned professionals reading this book. And to Christine Zuchora-Walske and Redleaf Press, thanks for always being there to offer guidance and support as we crafted the final version of this book.

Introduction

This book is written for both new and seasoned administrators who work in programs that provide care to children from birth through early adolescence. Child- and youth-serving programs come in all shapes and sizes, and the people who are responsible for the day-to-day operations of these programs are called by many names. (This book uses the terms *administrator* and *director* interchangeably.)

Whatever titles these people go by, few states offer them any specialized training. Some directors are promoted from the ranks of frontline staff. Some hold a child- or youth-related degree. While enthusiastic and well-meaning, administrators often come to their work with little or no management training. They may be wonderful teachers in the classroom and may have a passion for child- and youth-serving programs, but the skill set for an effective director is different from that of a classroom teacher. Often, new administrators do not even know the laws that govern hiring teachers or how to create a realistic budget. Facing many stumbling blocks and lacking information, new directors find their enthusiasm turning to stress and frustration. They may feel as if they are paddling upstream with a hole in their canoe.

This book's goal is to identify areas that new and seasoned administrators of child- and youth-serving programs find most challenging. Topics include empowering staff, creating an effective budget, balancing work and home, and much more. This book provides readers with information to consider when they confront job duties they find difficult or have never done, as well as "Tips from the Field" gathered through interviews with administrators across the country.

Whatever previous experience you have as an administrator, you know—or will soon realize—that a child- or youth-serving organization is like a three-ring circus, and you are the ringmaster. Jones Loflin and Todd Musig (2007, 31), authors of the book *Juggling Elephants*, propose that "the ringmaster has the greatest impact on the success of the circus." To be a good ringmaster, you need specific skills. This book will help you build those skills. Its user-friendly text outlines realistic situations and appropriate solutions. It is designed to provide a well-rounded, step-by-step instructional guide to help you become an effective and successful child care administrator.

PART 1

Walking on a New Path

You are the boss now. The balloons are gone, and the celebration dinner is over. It is time to get to work, making this role your own. You are probably both excited and nervous to begin. Whether you have extensive experience, are a first-time director or administrator, or are brand-new to an organization, you may find that your new role can be overwhelming and confusing. You might be torn between what you knew to be true in your previous position and the reality of your new job.

If you were promoted from within your organization, you will soon realize that you have access to information you didn't have before. You may now better understand why the administration made certain unpopular decisions. You may find it difficult to interact with the people with whom you once discussed the strengths and weaknesses of your boss and organization. As the new boss, how do you remain friends with staff you now supervise?

The reality is the dynamics of your friendship will change, but you can still be friends. Have a conversation with your colleagues. Explain how your new role limits sharing of information. Be truthful about what you can and cannot discuss. Make sure your friends know that your door is always open and that you will be there to listen to them. Let them know that you value them and you want to include them in solving problems when they occur. Navigating this change in relationships can be challenging, but it does not have to be painful. It helps if you are honest and straightforward from the start.

Change, while inevitable, is one of the most difficult things to cope with in life. Most people like the status quo, as it is predictable and comfortable. Change becomes easier to handle if trust exists among all parties involved. In fact, staff trust is required for successful progress. Without trust, a program can implode. With trust, a program can flourish. As Stephen M. R. Covey (2006, 285), the author of *The Speed of Trust*, says, "The dividends of trust can significantly enhance the quality of every relationship on every level of your life."

Transparency is the first step in developing trust, and honesty is the cornerstone of transparency. Trust or mistrust can develop at the speed of light. Those affected by a change need to understand from the outset that the change is being made to benefit all concerned. The effectiveness of your communication about change can mean the difference between trust and mistrust during the transition. Think of a time when you thought people understood what you were trying to do or say, while in reality, they misunderstood it completely. Such misunderstandings can lead to wariness on the part of employees. Be honest about what you currently know and do not know. Employees will respect you more if you say you do not know something than if you make up an answer to satisfy them and then backpedal when you find out the answer you gave was incorrect.

At times, ethics or lack of a decision will prevent you from answering a question. In the latter case, you can say, "I am still working on that, and I will get back to you when a decision is made." If ethics are limiting your ability to respond, you could reply, "I was not given permission to share that with you," or "I am not at liberty to share that with you." These short sentences give honest answers as to why you cannot share information while maintaining your professional integrity.

Respect is another key aspect of building trust. You do not have to agree with staff on everything. But you should respect them enough to listen to their concerns and fears about change, their suggestions about what needs to be changed, and their suggestions for implementing change.

If you have been a director at another organization, your learning curve for the overall job responsibilities may be smaller than if you are a rookie director. But you'll need to resist the temptation to quickly change things to how you have always done them. Rapid change can create difficulty with staff and families. You will need to take it slow, and patience will be your best ally. Take time to learn what is acceptable within this organization, understand regulations that govern this program, and determine employees' individual skills. This approach will allow you to understand what works well and what needs to be changed. Involving families and staff when you make changes will benefit all.

If this is your first job as a director, and you have never spent time doing the job of those you now supervise, you will need to put in some time observing and learning from your staff while identifying their skills. It is easy to let past experiences cloud your judgment about current employees. You will need to put on new, unbiased glasses as you observe how your coworkers perform their jobs and as you identify their skills. In addition, you will need to take time to understand the regulations that govern your organization. Have patience, flexibility, a listening ear, an open mind, and a willingness to learn. Observing and listening will give you a clear picture of how the organization runs and what skills your staff possess or lack.

To be a fair and effective director or administrator, it is important to understand the responsibilities of your current role. You may be familiar with some of them, but there will also be duties you have never or rarely done (such as things that happen only once a year). So, the fact is you will not know how to do everything you're responsible for until you've completed a full year in your new role. Preparation, patience, and taking it slow will ease your transition into this role for you, staff, children, and families alike.

Understanding Your New Role

*It's not what you achieve in life that defines you,
it's what you overcome.*

**CARLTON FISK, NATIONAL BASEBALL HALL OF FAME
INDUCTION SPEECH**

Getting promoted to an administrator position or becoming an administrator at a new organization can be an exciting event that demonstrates your overall competency. Along with feelings of excitement and pride often come stress and uneasiness. You are now in a position to make new, large-scale organizational, programmatic, and environmental differences in the lives of children, staff, and families. You can see for yourself just how much more the job is than taking prospective clients on a tour of the program, talking on the phone, or attending meetings outside the program. You may be spending more and more time at work, because nothing ever seems finished. Or you may feel overwhelmed and unsure where to start, knowing that how you conduct yourself in these first days will foster trust or mistrust with your staff and families. These are all normal reactions. Every new job has a learning curve. Let's simply start at the beginning and develop an understanding of job descriptions. This is the foundation for doing your job effectively.

JOB DESCRIPTIONS

In your interview or orientation, you should have received a job description. However, you may have spent little or no time going over the job description. This is a road map you will use to do your job, so take time to review it line by line so you understand exactly what is expected of you. Taking time now to review this document will help you avoid missed deadlines and confusion about expectations and timelines.

As you review your job description, highlight in green everything you currently feel comfortable doing without direction. Use blue to highlight responsibilities for which you have some knowledge but also need some direction. Finally, if you have no clue what a duty is or how to complete it, highlight it in yellow. This color-coded job description can serve as the basis for a role-clarity meeting with your supervisor.

List each responsibility on a separate piece of paper, color-coded as described above. Often, job descriptions list broad duties, such as "responsible for hiring and firing employees." This duty actually represents many tasks. To clarify exactly what is expected under each job duty, list the tasks that you feel are components of that duty, leaving space for other tasks your supervisor might add. Then write questions you'd like to ask, leaving space for notes and deadlines. Job descriptions typically do not list deadlines, so asking about them will help you get things done proactively rather than reactively. Knowing what is expected ahead of time beats finding out something needs to be done the next day.

Now you're ready to schedule a role-clarity meeting with your supervisor. You may find this meeting stressful, but it will help you with planning, which will prevent even more stress—and possibly missed deadlines—later. When you arrive at the meeting, have your questions on hand, and be ready to take notes.

Start by reviewing duties you feel comfortable with (highlighted in green). Confirm how and when those things need to be completed. For example, let's say you know that you need to review each week's lesson plans by the preceding Wednesday. You may want to know if you have flexibility to change that day. If you want to make a change to a deadline or process, be prepared to give your reasons for the change and to accept any reasons the change cannot happen. Note deadlines where applicable, areas in which you have flexibility, areas or processes your boss would like you to revamp, and to whom (if anyone) duties are currently delegated. Some duties may be delegated to off-site administrative staff. For instance, an outside company may generate all your paychecks, or an independent accountant may handle all your tax reporting. Introduce yourself to off-site service providers, and make sure you know when they need information from you and in what format they would like that information.

You may find yourself in a situation where your boss will allow you free rein to determine your own deadlines and processes. Before throwing out everything the organization has done in the past, take time to learn what it is currently doing and why, as well as the history behind that. You may find that the existing processes and deadlines work just fine. By preserving processes that already work well, you can reduce the stress of change for both staff and families.

Second, discuss the job duties for which you need some clarification (highlighted in blue). The clarification could be as simple as finding out where the organization typically purchases consumable classroom materials or if it has a membership to a local discount store for purchasing snacks. Ask about any pertinent deadlines or protocols. If after some conversation and clarification with your boss, you achieve comfort with the blue items, use the yellow highlighter to highlight over them so they turn green. Once again, make note of deadlines, flexibility, and changes your boss would like to see.

Next, review the items you don't know how to do (highlighted in yellow). It is always best to be truthful about what you know and do not know. This approach prevents misunderstandings and problems later, when something does not get done correctly or on time.

For example, let's say your organization has a company that cuts paychecks for your employees, but you are responsible for creating paperwork for the payroll company and getting it to them so your staff is paid on time. That means you are responsible for making sure the employees complete and submit time sheets—but you have never done time sheets before. Or, let's say it is your responsibility to cut the paychecks. You know how to cut checks, but you do not understand federal, state, and local payroll taxes or the forms, filing processes, and deadlines that accompany these taxes. In both cases, the smart thing to do is ask for information and coaching right off the bat.

In most job descriptions, you will find a statement similar to "duties as assigned." If you see this in your job description, ask your boss what types of duties have been assigned in the past under this statement. These may be duties that arose from some unforeseen issue, and they are not ongoing. If they are ongoing duties, then request that they be added to your job description so it accurately reflects your workload.

It is also important to discuss whether certain duties are delegated to others. Even though some duties, such as filing taxes or handling payroll, may be delegated to others, you can be sure you will need to do some tasks related to these duties, such as making sure all employees have filled out a W-9 form and submitting these forms to the accountant or payroll company. Though you may be unfamiliar with these tasks, and your boss knows you have a learning curve, the organization will still expect you to complete the tasks on time. When your responsibilities are clear, it's easier to execute them successfully.

What if you find yourself or a member of your staff without a job description? If you lack a job description, the first step is to meet with your boss. Discuss your boss's expectations, so you both have a clear idea of all the responsibilities your position has. This process takes time, so go slow, and make sure your job description is complete. Create a comprehensive list of responsibilities and deadlines. After you create it, review it and send it to your boss for review so that no misunderstandings about your duties occur.

If you find an employee without a job description or one that hasn't been reviewed in the past year, engage the person in the process of creating a job description. Have the employee make a comprehensive list of duties and responsibilities, working from an existing or outdated list if desired. Think about all the staff who have the same job title, and compare who is doing what. You may find some lead teachers who do more than others, or you may find that different assistant teachers take on different tasks in the classroom. It is up to you to create an inclusive job description for each title to which all staff with that title will adhere equally.

This process will allow you to create a job description that reflects the job responsibilities of each job type as accurately as possible. Once you have the list for each job, combine the tasks under headings. For example, for a director, one heading may be *marketing* and it may include such tasks as creating an updated program brochure, placing monthly ads in the local newspaper, and creating flyers to be handed out to human resources personnel in area businesses. For a teacher, one heading may be *lesson planning*, and it may include tasks such as identifying materials needed for the current lesson plan, purchasing required materials, and redesigning the environment to support the lesson plan.

In addition, many programs require employees to adhere to a professional code of ethics as part of their job duties. A code of ethics document helps guide an individual's conduct in accordance with primary values and ethical standards. Several national membership organizations have created codes of ethics for child- and youth-serving programs. They are the National Association for the Education of Young Children (NAEYC), the National AfterSchool Association (NAA), and the Association for Child and Youth Care Practice (ACYCP). The National Association for Family Child Care (NAFCC) uses the code of ethics written by NAEYC. If you are looking for a code of ethics for your organization, these have been legally reviewed and field-tested. Each will provide you with a comprehensive guidance tool when dealing with ethical situations.

Some programs have the staff sign their job descriptions. This signature verifies that the employee understands the document and knows the director will answer any employee questions. The signed document is placed in the staff member's personnel file. Appendix A contains several types of staff job descriptions and a statement of commitment to a code of ethics. If you create a two-way conversation about job descriptions with your boss and staff during this process, you will set the stage for effective ongoing communication and a clear understanding of expectations.

Tips from the Field

✓ Review job descriptions with staff once a year.

✓ Review job descriptions with new employees during orientation.

✓ Include "duties as assigned" at the bottom of all job descriptions.

✓ Create job descriptions for all staff.

✓ Regardless of the type of board your organization has (parent, advisory, or working), make sure board members understand their roles and expectations.

UNDERSTANDING DEADLINES

Now that you have a job description with clearly defined expectations and deadlines, you can plan your workday to get things completed in a timely manner. Look at the job description, and separate the duties into the following five categories: daily, weekly, monthly, quarterly, and yearly.

First, break down the daily and weekly duties into tasks. Estimate the time it takes to complete each task, so you can create a daily schedule made up of these tasks. For instance, once you know what time you need to get the lunch count to the cook each day, you can figure out when you will need to collect the count. You could delegate this task to the cook, freeing up time for you to do other tasks.

When you initially create your schedule, inflate the time needed to complete each task. Once you have a clear understanding of how long it really takes to complete each task, then revise your schedule. This strategy will give you time to master each task. Furthermore, interruptions are the rule when you're the director. You will rarely start and finish a task without some interruption. Something as simple as a telephone call can derail you. Building extra time into your daily schedule will reduce not only your personal stress but also your need to work extended hours.

Daily and weekly tasks are the easiest to schedule. They are also easiest to master because of their redundancy. They quickly become routine. Things get a little more difficult when you begin to add monthly tasks, such as food program documentation, subsidy paperwork, and board reports, into your schedule. You can make some of these tasks more manageable by splitting them into smaller tasks, such as tabulating the subsidy paperwork weekly instead of monthly.

Quarterly tasks, such as budgets or tax payments, are easy to forget because of their infrequency. Schedule time to address each quarterly task one week prior to the due date. This approach will put it in the forefront of your mind and allow you time to gather needed information for completing it on time.

Yearly tasks can be overwhelming if you have not set up strategies throughout the year to help you complete these tasks efficiently. For example, creating family tax statements is a gargantuan job if you try to do them all at once. Accounting software can help you generate these statements with a few keystrokes. When you enter families' weekly payments in the accounting system or into a spreadsheet program, you may be able to generate a report that lists each family who has made payments in a given year and the total amount paid. If you are still using paper and pencil to record family payments, then tabulate subtotals monthly and every six months. By keeping a running total in this way, you will minimize your work when the time comes to provide statements for your families. For an example of a family year-end tax statement, see appendix B.

Creating a clear schedule that allows you a reasonable amount of time to complete your tasks while understanding that interruptions are inevitable will increase your effectiveness and decrease your stress. For a sample work grid that outlines some common tasks throughout the year, see appendix C.

Tips from the Field

✓ Make sure deadlines are realistic.

✓ Make note on the calendar one month prior to the deadline for a bigger task, such as a funder's quarterly report, so you can plan accordingly to meet the deadline.

✓ Alert staff about deadlines early enough for them to meet the deadlines.

✓ Give periodic reminders for long-range projects to help staff be successful and timely.

DELEGATION

No one person could accomplish all the tasks associated with running a child- or youth-serving organization. Delegation is the key to success. Delegation helps staff buy in to the organization and its mission and believe that they are an integral part of making the organization a great place. Be sure to consider employees' skills in order to increase proficiency and ownership. When you decide to delegate, include the following key elements:

- Provide guidance.
- State expected outcomes clearly.
- Set timelines for completion.
- Plan a time to check in.

Delegating a task should send the message that you believe the person can complete the task effectively. Take care to send this message clearly. You do not want employees to feel that delegated tasks are just additional work. Understanding your staff's individual strengths and using this knowledge to delegate tasks to those who have the appropriate skills will go a long way toward effective completion.

When you delegate a task, you need to be able to let it go—allow your staff to complete the task. Don't micromanage it. Not everyone will complete a given task the way you might. Everyone has strengths and weaknesses. Begin by looking at the task's end goal. Then ask yourself, "How will I know the task has been completed effectively?" Provide guidance, clearly communicate expected outcomes and parameters such as deadlines and spending limits, and list nonnegotiable elements of the task. Tell the employee that you are available, and make a date to check in prior to the deadline.

For example, let's say the delegated task is to create a weekly lesson plan that meets all the guidelines set by the licensing agency or national accreditation standards for lesson plans. Indicate the deadline will be the Wednesday before the week the lesson plan is to be used. State how much money can be spent on additional supplies for the lesson activities. Nonnegotiable elements may be that the employee must use a prescribed form and that each activity needs to list the specific licensing or accreditation standard. Let the employee work within the parameters you give, then step back and see what the employee accomplishes. When you check in with the employee, you can ask questions for clarification or request expansion of an idea. You might find that the employee is having a hard time accomplishing the task; if some coaching is needed, provide it.

You can find more information on and examples of task delegation in chapter 2.

Tips from the Field

- ✓ Match staff skills and interests with tasks to be delegated.

- ✓ Resist the temptation to micromanage.

- ✓ Trust your employees to do their jobs.

- ✓ Just because it is not your way does not mean it is a bad way.

- ✓ Monitor progress, provide guidance, and intercede only when necessary.

- ✓ Acknowledge a job well done.

2

Leadership

Leadership is the art of accomplishing more than the science of management says is possible.

COLIN POWELL, *A SOLDIER'S WAY*

The words *leadership* and *management* are sometimes used interchangeably. But they don't really have the same meaning. According to Merriam-Webster's dictionary, leadership is guiding others, while management is making decisions about a business or other organization. US Navy Rear Admiral Grace Hopper said it best: "You don't manage people; you manage things. You lead people" (Cutler 2015, 88). Administrators use both skills to succeed, but this chapter will focus on leadership.

LEADERSHIP SKILLS

Leaders have a vision of future goals and the ability to motivate others to achieve those goals. Leaders communicate their goals, identify staff skills, provide the needed tools and resources, and stand back and allow their staff to make things happen. Effective leaders use many skills to accomplish the goals they set. Some of these skills are communication, delegation, guidance, accessibility, and collaboration.

In any leadership position, effective communication is an essential skill. Communication is more than talking; it is the exchange of information that includes speaking, listening, and clarification. Reading body language and the tone of a conversation is an important aspect of communication, too. These cues can tell us a lot about the emotional context of a topic among a specific group of people.

Written communication is especially important in the electronic age. Information written in an e-mail, for example, should always be professional and concise. Incorrect grammar or use of the caps lock key will change the entire tone of a written communication. Once an e-mail has been sent, the sender loses all control of it. For a more detailed discussion of effective communication, please see chapter 5.

When you're the director, it is tempting to micromanage every project or situation. After all, you are the boss, and whatever the staff does reflects on you, right? Wrong. Your goal as an administrator is to lead people to successful task completion. In other words, it's important to delegate. Over the long haul, fostering independent thinking and self-motivation will create a team that supports new initiatives with a can-do attitude. Naturally, you already know that this is always your goal. But sometimes it is hard to let go and let staff get the job done.

Understanding your staff's skills will help you know what tasks you can delegate. It also allows you to acknowledge and tap into those skills, empower staff, and provide opportunities for them to grow and shine. When employees feel you appreciate their skills and contributions, they are more likely to be happy and want to come to work.

Once you have decided to delegate a task, you will need to offer guidance. First, you need to know and articulate what the successfully completed task looks like. In addition, you will need to communicate the goal of the task, any guidelines, a deadline for completion, and elements that are nonnegotiable. For example, you might decide you would like a particular employee to take the lead in creating a family night. This employee expressed at a recent staff meeting that a family night would be a great way to introduce changes in the family handbook, and you know this person is organized and creative. Before you meet to request the employee's participation, you need to know the answers to the following questions:

- In what month do you want to have the family night?
- What nights are you unavailable during that month?
- How much money has been allocated for the event?
- Will there be food at the event?
- What do you hope the families will learn?
- Will child care be available?
- When would you like to have an update about the progress of this event?

By taking time to think through these questions, you will accomplish two important things. First, you will get a clear idea of what you really want and what limitations exist. Second, you will be able to communicate the scope of the task and provide information and resources to complete the task. Meet with the employee to convey this information. Give clear parameters and expectations, as well as a time to check in with you. End the meeting by inviting the employee to ask questions if trouble crops up prior to the check-in date.

Now comes the hard part: without micromanaging, sit back, and let the employee complete the task. It may not be done exactly the way you would do it. But when the task is done, you need to ask yourself, Was a family night planned as requested? Did it come in under or at budget? Did it meet the need of introducing changes to the family handbook? If *yes* is the answer to all these questions, then the delegated task has been a success.

Often, when you let staff lead, they come up with creative solutions that you may not have considered. Trusting your staff to complete a given task is essential to developing positive, supportive interpersonal relationships. You empower employees by believing in their ability to complete the task effectively and on time. Your confidence in them creates a can-do attitude. It encourages staff to believe that working together, they can solve any problem. Growing leaders is an ongoing part of your job. When staff are successful, so are you.

Being accessible and approachable is key to developing good relationships with staff. Just as you need to know your staff, your staff needs to know you. Schedule routine check-in meetings with individual employees, even if for only a few minutes. You might discuss what has happened recently that has made the employee feel happy to be working in your program. You could also use this time to check in about the employee's family, issues at work, ways to provide support, how a given project is going, or just to say thanks for a job well done.

Make sure staff know when you will be in the building, as well as times when you will be unavailable, such as when you will be conducting a scheduled tour. Being accessible during program hours when you are in the building or by phone when you are not in the building sends the message that employees are important and that you will make time for them. Reaching out to staff when you see they are troubled or just need an ear to vent can establish a mentor-mentee relationship. It says, "I am here if you need me."

Collaboration is another critical leadership skill. Being a collaborator can be hard, but its rewards are endless. As an administrator, you might often believe that because you are the boss with all the information, you should be making all the decisions. It's true that many times, you alone should make the decision. But even in those cases, inviting others to share ideas can be beneficial.

Your job as a leader is not to know all the answers but rather to know of existing resources and to inspire staff to educate themselves and generate appropriate solutions. As a person new to a particular administrative role, you may find that employees know more about a given situation than you do. Let yourself learn from them. You may find that when you give staff time to talk, they come up with great solutions and new ways of doing things.

When you communicate with staff, families, and community leaders that there is more than one way to accomplish a given task and include them in decision making, you create a collaborative environment. This environment excels when all parties begin with open minds and willingness to listen to others' ideas. Set the stage for success by laying down ground rules, identifying common goals, and stating that all ideas presented will be discussed.

A collaborative environment can begin with your staff meetings. Take time to plan meetings that are meaningful to staff, rather than meetings that feel like hours they will never get back. Planning is key. Create an agenda, and let your staff add agenda items prior to the meeting. If a staff member requests an agenda item, then place that person's name after that item. Ask what the person plans to discuss on that topic, so you can prepare. When that topic comes up at the meeting, let the employee who requested it take the floor.

Here are a few questions to ask yourself when you are creating a staff meeting agenda:

- What really needs to be covered at the meeting?

- How much time will each agenda item require?

- What is the purpose of the meeting—is it an informational, decision-making, or idea-generating meeting?

- Will the meeting have more than one purpose?

- Is the meeting necessary? If not, then cancel it.

Once the agenda is complete, distribute it to your staff before the meeting. If employees need to bring something to the meeting, remind them when you distribute the agenda. Let them know how much time will be devoted to the meeting. When possible, delegate tasks for the meeting, such as assembling the agenda, taking minutes, keeping the group on topic (serving as topic master), setting up the meeting space, and buying snacks. Rotating these tasks among staff helps you establish a sense of purpose.

Throughout this book, you will find many ideas for staff meeting topics. Here are some standard items for discussion that you can include in your staff meeting agendas:

- budget update

- staffing update

- accreditation update

- Quality Rating and Improvement System (QRIS) update

- enrollment update

- building space usage update

- policy update

- training topics wanted or available

- upcoming events
- recap
- roles assigned for next meeting
- next meeting date

In addition to agenda topics, staff meetings can include training. If you plan to do training during a staff meeting, tell staff in advance. The meeting agenda should indicate the name of the training as well as the additional time that the training will take.

During the meeting, take care to keep the group on topic. Explain in your ground rules that if the meeting veers off topic, the topic master will steer the group back on topic. This approach will establish expectations for the discussion and limit the feeling of not being heard. If a topic needs more time, then place the item on a future agenda so that more time can be devoted to the discussion. Be aware that an individual who is passionate about a subject may dominate the conversation. Make sure everyone gets a chance to speak.

A well-planned meeting can be a great way to provide program updates and include staff in program decision making and problem solving. Here are a few more tips for planning and running staff meetings:

- Include staff in preparing the agenda for a staff meeting.
- If you have nothing to discuss in an upcoming meeting that's new or different from the last one, cancel the meeting.
- Make sure you have written information in front of you for each agenda item.
- Have meeting ground rules written and posted.
- Stick to the time you have allocated for a staff meeting.
- Choose your next meeting date before leaving the current meeting.
- Take attendance at each meeting, and make it part of your minutes.
- At the bottom of the minutes, list task assignments for the next meeting.
- Write up and distribute staff meeting minutes promptly.

Collaboration with staff encourages them to think creatively to establish new policies or reach out to community partners to provide activities. If you stay within your own head or within the walls of your program, never venturing out to see what others think or how others do things, you will soon be scratching your head and wondering why your vision for the program isn't becoming a reality. When you sincerely open the dialogue to gather new ideas and approaches, you create a dynamic and effective partnership while developing ownership in the program. Leading is not always easy, but when you empower staff to excel, you will see them fly—and that is a wonderful thing to behold.

Tips from the Field

✓ Remember that leaders are forged, not born. Becoming a leader takes time, pain, pressures, challenges, and being open to other ways.

✓ Do not get involved in interpersonal conflicts until you have talked to all parties.

✓ Listen first, talk second.

✓ Keep in mind that leaders provide opportunities, skills, and recognition.

✓ Expect to make mistakes. The goal is to learn from them. Remember that every winner has fallen down at some point.

✓ Be flexible in everything.

CHANGING PERCEPTIONS AND ESTABLISHING CREDIBILITY

If you have worked in your organization before in a different capacity, then staff and families will already have an opinion of you, your work ethic, and how you treat people. Your experience is a double-edged sword. While it is nice to know your colleagues and how the organization works, you are now in a different role, and you will need to prove you belong there, even to your closest allies.

Some people go into this new job like a bull in a china shop, changing and "improving" processes left and right. Others stand by meekly, not wanting to upset anyone or anything. A third approach lies somewhere in between. Using the third approach offers you the opportunity and time to determine what changes work best for you, children, families, staff, and the organization.

Perceptions do not change overnight. Just because you have a title does not mean you have everyone's respect or confidence. These come over time as staff, families, and children watch you in action. People always say that children see more than adults give them credit for. Staff and families are no different. While they may not say anything, they do watch how you treat people and how you conduct yourself.

Your new position should not change who you are, but it will change how you respond to things. One director advises that regardless of how you are being treated, you should treat everyone with respect and acceptance for who they are and where they came from. According to another director, you cannot be friends with your staff and families, but you can be friendly. You may find yourself in the same social or community groups with staff members and families outside of work. If this occurs, it is important to have a frank conversation with them. Explain that you can't discuss work issues outside of work, regardless of how long you have known that person. Making this statement up front can establish some clear boundaries; however, it will be up to you to maintain those boundaries. Once the lines get blurred, it is hard to go back to a no-work-outside-work policy.

You also may find yourself faced with staff or families expecting special treatment. How can you deal with this tricky situation? Look first to your written policy. Do you have a policy dictating what steps you should take? If not, ask yourself, Would I do this for all my employees or families? Will others perceive this as favoritism? Without a doubt, others will be watching to see how you handle things. Both families and staff want an administrator who is fair and consistent. If you have to decline the request, you will need to be direct. Explain that while you are a friend, in your new position, you cannot grant the request. Take time to explain why. Is it financial or logistical? If you have a policy that prevents you from granting the request, refer to it. If one does not exist, you may need to add a policy about that type of request.

For example, let's say an employee who is a friend wants a day off on short notice. The program policy states that a request form for a day off must be submitted a week prior to the day needed. You would need to decline the request due to your program's policy. If the employee needs only a few hours off, you might offer her other options. Perhaps she could change shifts with someone else on staff or ask if someone would be willing to work later to cover her shift. If the employee is facing an unexpected emergency, you could try to get a sub for her or work her shift.

Whether you were promoted from within your program or hired from outside, you will need to prove you have what it takes to do the job effectively. In other words, you need to establish credibility. Credibility is being believable, capable, and trustworthy. Establishing credibility is an ongoing process. Your past reputation, good or bad, will follow you. If you were hired from outside, the staff will want to know more about you. Share information about your education and past employment to assure staff that you can do the job. Be aware that people will look to online sources such as Facebook and LinkedIn to see what you say about yourself and others.

Whether you were hired from within or were an outside candidate, employees need to know you can make the transition, so show them. Be professional and accessible. Ask questions when you are unsure about something. Engage staff and the community in the organization. This will help them experience how you operate, see your credentials, and witness your ability to relate and communicate with others. Engagement will go a long way toward establishing your credibility. People want to see you up close and find out what you are made of. They want to know you are fair, compassionate, and willing to listen. If you engage them in the day-to-day running of the program, then you will develop buy-in to the program. When a problem arises, engaging staff and families in finding solutions helps them become part of a positive process rather than part of the problem.

Tips from the Field

✓ Changing perceptions about your ability takes time.

✓ People will think what they want to think; you can only provide them with information to change their minds.

✓ Managing by reputation only does not work. Establishing credibility happens when you show people, rather than tell them, what your capabilities are.

✓ How you handle a sticky situation will say volumes about your credibility.

Outlining New Expectations

The real leader has no need to lead—he is content to point the way.

HENRY MILLER, *THE WISDOM OF THE HEART*

After you have taken time to understand your role, it's time to roll up your sleeves and gain a clear understanding about how your program operates. Once again, you will need to put on a set of unbiased glasses and look at the program from a variety of angles. You may find that you need to make changes. If so, go slow. Staff and families know that every change in management will bring changes in programming, policies, and procedures. They simply want you to be thoughtful and careful when making changes. Because each change is bound to create some angst, it is important to take your time when you're deciding whether and how to make a change. As long as children and staff are safe, there's no hurry. Examining how a change may affect various aspects of the program takes time and an openness to look objectively at each area of programming.

FINANCIAL REVIEW

Look first at the overall financial health and stability of the program. If you find a clear deficit, you can begin making changes to eliminate the shortfall. Your job description should tell you what your role is in developing an operating budget, maintaining costs within line items, and inputting revenues and expenses within a budget tracking system. Whether you or another individual is responsible for creating or monitoring a budget, you should reflect on the following questions:

- How does the program's revenue compare with its expenses? Are you bringing in more money than you are spending per month?

- Are you able to pay your monthly bills on time?

- Is your program expected to make a certain amount of profit, or is your program a nonprofit?

- What funding streams does your program currently have?

- Does the program have a line of credit?

- Does the program have a savings account?

- Does the program use a credit card?

- Overall, is the program in the black or in the red?

Even if you are not the person responsible for budgeting, it is still important for you to understand what your budget is each month and what flexibility you have within the budget to reallocate funds to meet certain needs. Determining whether the program is financially stable will let you know when changes need to be made within the program and just how much money you have to make those changes. For a more detailed discussion of budgeting, please see chapter 8.

Tips from the Field

✔ Understand the accounting terms used within your organization.

✔ Make time to review the budget regularly.

✔ Review funding stream expenditure policies.

REVIEWING RULES, REGULATIONS, AND POLICIES

Now that you have reviewed your program's financials, it is time to look at the requirements of any regulatory agencies that govern your program. In addition to licensing requirements, your program may also have requirements from agencies such as local building, fire, zoning, and health departments. Call these agencies and make sure you know what the current requirements are and how to comply with them.

It is wise to pay special attention to state licensing requirements. If you were promoted from within your organization, do not rely on your memory or on what someone has told you. Refer directly to the licensing agency. While not all states have licensing requirements for all ages of children, it is important that you know what is required of you as a new administrator and what is required of your program. For instance, make sure your name is listed as administrator on the program license. Submit paperwork and education verification as soon as you assume the administrator's position. This approach can eliminate issues when you receive an inspection visit. Review any noncompliance reports issued to your program, and make sure changes were made so the program is now in compliance. For more on how to review current licensing regulations, please see chapter 15.

After you've studied all applicable rules and regulations, it's time to review your program's handbooks and orientation materials for both staff and families. See what your written policies really say. Often, these documents are not updated regularly, so you may find outdated information in them. If you do, make a note to update the documents to reflect your current policies. In addition, make notes about policies that are not in the handbook and should be, as well as those that no longer apply. For instance, if your program used to have daily access to a swimming pool but no longer offers daily swimming, then remove all related policy statements. If a policy seems unclear, flag it for staff review and possible rewriting or deletion. For a more detailed discussion of handbooks, please see chapter 12.

Tips from the Field

✔ Include handbook items for review as part of your staff meeting.

✔ Ask questions about policies that seem outdated or are no longer in use.

✔ Review the licensing regulations as they relate to parent and staff handbook topics.

PROFESSIONAL DEVELOPMENT

As you review regulatory agency requirements, you will learn what professional development each regulatory agency demands, such as the type and amount of training each type of employee needs. For instance, if your program is nationally accredited or part of a statewide Quality Rating and Improvement System (QRIS), your staff will require more training than your state or local licensing requires. It is also important to make sure that you know the specific types of training required, such as a class on child abuse, a class on child assessment, or a management class. Armed with this information, you can review each staff file and determine who is in compliance and who needs additional training. Be aware that sometimes specific types of training are hard to find. Devoting time to informing yourself about the type and amount of training needed by each employee will allow you time to schedule training before your next monitoring visit or inspection.

Tips from the Field

✔ Create a spreadsheet that keeps track of the professional development all staff receive so you can quickly determine the total hours of training for each employee.

✔ Place a cover sheet within each staff file that documents ongoing professional development, and attach documentation of attendance to this cover sheet so it is easy to review.

✔ Provide staff with quarterly reminders of how many hours they have achieved toward their yearly requirement.

✔ Through e-mail and staff meetings, remind employees about the expectation to obtain ongoing professional development.

ORGANIZATION HISTORY

To understand and appreciate the history of your organization, meet with all staff members individually to learn how they perceive the program, what they believe works well, and what they believe does not work. Taking time to look at how things are being done currently will prevent you from reinventing the wheel or repeating unsuccessful strategies. Staff will know how your predecessor did things. Have a one-on-one chat with each staff member to ask the following questions:

- What do you like best about working here?
- If you had to name just one skill at which you excel, what would it be?
- What is your favorite part of your job?
- What should I know about you?
- What do you think is important for me to know about the program?
- If you could do one thing differently in the program, what would it be and why?
- How do you prefer to communicate—face-to-face, by text, by e-mail, in writing, or some other way?
- How and when would you like to see staff meetings held?
- What is your preferred type of professional development (in-house, online, all-day, evening, all-staff in-service days, or other)?

Asking each employee these questions and others you feel are important gives you a great idea of what each person needs to be proficient. It also provides you with staff-specific views on themselves and the program. It begins a process of including staff in program assessment, growth, and problem solving.

Tips from the Field

✓ Hold one-on-one meetings outside the office whenever possible. Employees tend to feel more open and less stressed away from the workplace.

✓ Take ten minutes per employee per week to check in face-to-face. These check-ins are great opportunities to compliment staff on work well done.

✓ Getting to know your staff on a personal level helps you support them when life challenges crop up.

✓ Be truthful about all aspects of staff job expectations.

✓ Build trust so employees feel comfortable coming to you with concerns.

✓ It is easy to become overwhelmed in a new administrative position, so give yourself a chance to acclimate. Take time to review what has been done and what needs to be done.

CLASSROOM AND PROGRAMMING OBSERVATIONS

Change is inevitable. But too much change too soon could cause a staff revolt. To avoid too-rapid change, take your time getting to know the community, environment, and dynamics of each classroom.

Observation is a great way to get firsthand knowledge about what is happening in each classroom. It is important to tell staff you are coming for the first observation, so they don't feel ambushed. Make it clear you will be a wallflower during the observation. Tell employees that you will meet with them later to talk about the observation.

When you meet with staff, be sure to tell them that your questions are an avenue to understand their thought process, not an indication that you dislike or disagree with what you observed. Explain that because you are new to your role as an administrator, you do not have background information on why certain procedures and practices were formed, and that your questions will help you fill in the blanks.

Ask questions for clarification, such as, "Tell me why you do it that way," or "Help me understand why you do that this way." An employee may respond, "Well, that is just the way we do it." If that happens, just keep asking questions. Inquire, "What is the goal of that particular practice?" When you ask that question, it makes people think about why they do what they are doing. For your part, do not disregard staff experiences; rather, take time to understand why they do things the way they do.

Asking open-ended questions and involving staff in problem solving can empower them. For example, during one observation, a director noticed that all the children came into the program, lined up, and went to the restroom to wash their hands and use the bathroom if needed. The children reentered the program, where many centers, including a snack table, were located around the room. The children moved freely from space to space. When the director asked the staff why all the children lined up to wash hands when they entered the program, the employees responded, "We have always done it that way." So the director asked, "What is the purpose of that practice?" The staff answered, "The children need to have clean hands for snack." The director noted that that was a worthwhile goal and also pointed out that only six children out of thirty-six chose snack before playing at a center. The staff were floored. They felt reassured that their goal was on target but now saw that their practice fell short of their goal. This knowledge empowered them to improve their practice.

Next, you will want to look at day-to-day programming. Does each employee have an up-to-date job description? How do staff create and document appropriate daily lesson plans? How do they order supplies? How do they document children's progress? How do they communicate with families?

Most new directors let their program run at status quo for several months at first, unless a safety or regulatory noncompliance needs to be addressed immediately. If you find such an issue, analyze the situation, and make immediate changes. Inform staff and families of the changes. Explain why the changes need to happen immediately.

When the time comes for broader programmatic or organizational change, you must be able to articulate clearly to staff and families why you feel the change is necessary. For example, let's say your predecessor wanted lesson plans one week prior to use. But you feel that does not give you enough time to order the needed supplies, provide guidance in implementing the lesson plans, or provide outside resources to support the activities. Present your reasons for moving to a monthly schedule.

You may already have an idea of how you want to change a process, but it is important to involve your staff in reviewing your plan and to engage them in tweaking the process for everyone's benefit. Once the process has run through several cycles, meet with staff again, and see if any adjustments need to be made. When the process is finalized, change your staff or family handbook to reflect the new or changed policy or procedure.

This way of making changes may seem arduous. However, the benefits of buy-in and understanding go a long way toward creating a cohesive work group.

Tips from the Field

✓ Involving staff in the change process is a great way to establish buy-in.

✓ Be open to staff's ideas and solutions.

✓ Before making any change, determine whether the change will affect other procedures or processes.

✓ Remember that change is hard for everyone.

✓ Do not expect miracles overnight; change takes time.

✓ Keep in mind that some people never accept change graciously.

Working with Boards

Feedback has to be built into the decision to provide continuous testing, against actual events, of the expectations that underlie the decision.

PETER F. DRUCKER, *MANAGEMENT: TASKS, RESPONSIBILITIES, PRACTICES*

To work effectively with your board, you need to both understand board dynamics and comprehend the purpose and duties of your board. Boards come in all shapes and sizes, and their roles can vary greatly. Some boards are figureheads; they get a report once a month and do little else. Other boards have responsibilities such as fundraising or establishing policies and procedures. Some boards are made up of a combination of community leaders and parents; others include professionals such as lawyers, marketing executives, or owners of local businesses; while still others are composed chiefly of parents and other family members. Boards can be your greatest ally and also your biggest challenge. If you have never reported to a board before, be honest about that with your colleagues.

BOARD OF DIRECTORS

If you report to a board of directors who oversee your organization, take some time to read the bios of board members. These bios will offer insight into the background of the board members and will tell you how long they have served.

Next, read the board members' job description and the meeting minutes from the past six meetings. These documents will outline what's important to the board and reveal the format in which its members like to receive their information. In addition, minutes will outline past issues, tell you how the board solved those issues, and indicate what has been tabled for future conversation.

Call and introduce yourself to each board member prior to attending your first meeting. This call will give you an opportunity to tell members a little about yourself and give them a chance to ask you questions before meeting you face-to-face. Follow up with a short note or e-mail thanking each board member for taking time to talk with you. This tells them that you appreciate the work they have done, and it helps convey that you are looking forward to working with them in the future. To keep them informed and engaged in your program, add all board members to your newsletter mailing list.

When you're preparing for your first board meeting, call the board chair and ask about the meeting format and typical things board members like reported. The chair may be able to give you a past report to use as a template. Also ask if there is any specific information the chair would like to see in future reports. The answers to these questions will indicate how formal your report needs to be.

Create a board binder or file, and place all board-specific items in it. This binder or file is a great place to put information throughout the month for inclusion in your board report, so everything is in one place when you create your report. Armed with the knowledge you've gathered, create a one-page summary of the information requested, and then add any other information you feel would be important for board members to know. Also create an up-to-date budget expenditure spreadsheet, even if it wasn't requested. This strategy shows board members that you are a good steward of the money and are closely tracking all expenditures. Make sure you are able to explain all expenditures. Make enough copies of your report and spreadsheet so you can give one to each board member and keep one for your own binder or file. Come early to the meeting to greet the board members and formally introduce yourself.

Tips from the Field

✓ Choose your board members well. Be aware of individuals who just want to put something on their résumé rather than be an active member of the board.

✓ Be able to defend your practices and budget.

✓ Get to know your board members, and include them in ongoing communications.

PARENT ADVISORY BOARD

Parent advisory boards are usually composed of parents or other family members of past and currently enrolled children, as well as current staff. Like a board of directors, a parent advisory board may either be a figurehead or play an active role in your program. The parent advisory board may have started as part of an accreditation process or QRIS requirement.

When you're working with a parent advisory board, it is important to introduce yourself to the members and get to know them prior to your first meeting. Calling them or meeting them face-to-face as they pick up their children conveys that you are glad to meet them and appreciate their dedication and service to the program. If a parent advisory board meeting is not scheduled within the first month of your new job, set one up. Make it casual, so you can check in with the members and get to know what they have been charged with doing.

For parent advisory boards to work effectively, they need guidelines, projects, and goals. If you find that these don't exist for your group, or you don't have a parent advisory board and would like to create one, here are a few things to consider:

- Develop clear expectations and guidelines.
- Clearly state the parent advisory board's role.
- What are the board's limitations?
- What projects can the group work on?
- What is the timeline for project completion?
- How often should the board meet?

Developing a board just for the sake of having one is a waste of your time and the board members' time, so you need to know what you expect the board to do and what you do not want it to do. For example, let's say you want your advisory group to research fundraising opportunities and choose one to conduct. But you do not want the board to make changes in any classroom. Deciding what the scope of the group's work will be is essential in creating a functional parent advisory board. Provide the board with guidance along the way. That means you will need to either attend meetings or assign a staff member to attend in your stead. Let members decide when they can meet, working around their own job schedules, or if they will use e-mail to communicate. If they choose the latter, ask to be included in their e-mail communications.

A parent advisory board is a great way to engage families and develop family ownership within your program. It can also help you tap into a volunteer workforce. It takes a little planning and guidance to keep the board on track, but the rewards can be invaluable.

Tips from the Field

✓ When you're working with parent advisory boards, give members clear expectations.

✓ Tap into and be open to the parent advisory board's ideas. A good idea can come from anywhere.

✓ Go after the loudest dissenters, and win them over. They will be your biggest advocates.

Effective Communication

The speed of communications is wondrous to behold.
It is also true that speed can multiply the distribution
of information that we know to be untrue.

EDWARD R. MURROW, FAMILY OF MAN
AWARD ACCEPTANCE SPEECH

Communication is essential in building relationships. Effective communication can be the cornerstone of a high-quality program and supportive relationships with families and staff. It is the cement in a cohesive team that operates with one voice and focus. Communication is a two-way street. It involves not only speaking but also listening, not only writing but also reading. Everyone communicates differently. While everyone uses words, the meanings individuals assign to words can be very different. For example, you may find the term *honey* endearing, but someone else may find it demeaning. Similarly, words like *respect* can mean different things to different people.

As an administrator, you need to know your employees and families so that you can avoid barriers to effective communication. Here are some common barriers:

- Emotions and stress can cause you to become overwhelmed and respond in an inappropriate way or present body language that's confusing to listeners.

- Not being present in a conversation, such as thinking about what you should be doing right now or will be doing in five minutes, can cause you to miss information or body language that's vital to addressing the issue at hand.

- When your words and body language are at odds, you send mixed messages. The listener can become confused and may not receive the intended message.

EMOTIONS

If either party in a conversation is experiencing strong emotions or stress, that can change the tone or meaning of a message. For example, when people feel targeted or unheard, their emotions may color the messages they hear or the responses they give.

It is okay to admit that a subject is very emotional to the speaker or listener. If emotions are getting in the way, take a few minutes to get a drink of water. Offer the other party water as well. This small time-out can help get the conversation back on track.

To restart the conversation (or begin a conversation) on the same page, ask a clarifying question. This strategy gives you time to think. Remember that it is okay to think before responding to a question or comment. Sometimes silence is a good thing.

At the end of the conversation, you may find it helpful to summarize the information exchanged, to make sure everyone understands. Once you have summarized, stop talking. There is no need to drag out the conversation.

ENGAGEMENT

When someone is talking, it is important to be fully engaged in listening and not trying to formulate your answer. Make eye contact, and nod occasionally to let the speaker know you are listening.

Wait until the speaker is finished speaking before you answer. Interrupting shows disrespect. When people feel disrespected by you, they are less likely to listen to you. If you interrupt, you may feel you are providing additional information or clarifying the information presented to you. But in reality, when you interrupt, you are not giving the speaker a chance to give you complete information. This could send the message that you think the speaker is wrong.

You don't need to agree with or even like the person with whom you are talking, but as an administrator, you need to be open to what the person has to say. It is in everyone's best interest for you to suppress the assignment of guilt or criticism until the speaker has had time to fully explain and you understand what he or she is trying to convey.

BODY LANGUAGE

Your body language, or nonverbal communication, can often tell the other person in a conversation how you really feel about the topic being discussed. Your body language includes your tone of voice, eye contact or lack thereof, how you stand, facial expressions such as eye rolling and smiling, as well as the position of your arms, such as uncrossed or crossed. Body language can tell others not only your feelings on a subject but also how engaged you are in it.

Reading body language to get a sense of emotions surrounding a conversation can help you respond appropriately. Remember that there will be individual differences in body language. People from different cultures may assign different meanings to various forms of nonverbal communication, so consider age, culture, gender, emotional state, and religion when you're reading someone's body language.

Tips from the Field

✔ Communication is key. Keep staff and families informed. Let them know how to reach you.

✔ Be consistent with information delivery. If a change is happening, let people know how it has changed from a previous communication.

✔ Providing a place for families, staff, and children to give you feedback creates opportunities to express ideas, ask questions, and identify issues that need to be addressed.

✔ Use many types of communication—paper, electronic, and spoken—with families and staff. Individuals hear things differently and have preferences about how they send and receive information.

✔ Communications should never be on pink paper. Some adults may have bad associations with pink slips (firing or layoff notices), so choose another paper color.

Marketing

Doing business without advertising is like winking at a girl in the dark. You know what you are doing, but nobody else does.

STEUART HENDERSON BRITT, *NEW YORK HERALD TRIBUNE*

Marketing is advertising, promoting, and selling your organization's services. The American Marketing Association (AMA 2013) defines marketing as "the activity, set of institutions, and processes for creating, communicating, delivering, and exchanging offerings that have value for customers, clients, partners, and society at large." Marketing can take many forms. It is important to develop a plan that clearly defines what you want and how you'll make that happen. Marketing needs to happen continuously and be reviewed regularly, not just when you want to fill a few empty slots or hire a new employee. So how do you begin?

UNDERSTANDING YOUR CUSTOMERS

Customers look for programs that meet their needs. So, the first step in creating an effective marketing strategy is understanding your customers. Knowing where your customers live, go to school, shop, worship, socialize, and get their information can help you generate a targeted geographical area in which to market your program. Once you know where your customers are located, you will need to discover what they want from a child- or youth-serving program. Surveying current families can help you assemble a list of items families need or want. Here are some things customers might need or want:

- transportation to the program
- hours of operation that meet their job hours

- meals and snacks provided
- affordability
- accreditation
- participation in state QRIS
- subsidy acceptance
- degreed staff
- inclusive policies
- summer programs
- regulatory agency licensure

Once you know your customers' needs, you can create marketing materials that communicate how your program meets these needs. Communicating how your program meets the needs of children and their families helps families make informed decisions about where to place their children. For example, if families want to know what type of education your employees have, then tell them. Some programs will say that a certain percentage of their staff have a two-year degree or higher. While this type of information can become out of date easily, it is important to convey that your program strives to maintain a specific percentage of degreed staff, because more and more states are requiring staff to be degreed or to have some formal education. If you currently are not within the percentage you have communicated, by using a word like *strive*, you communicate that your intent is to reach that percentage. It is equally important to state what type of degrees your employees have, such as child development, early childhood, or elementary education. Placing copies of staff diplomas and certificates outside each classroom is another great marketing tool.

Tips from the Field

✓ Do not assume that your customer understands all the child and youth regulations you need to follow within your state.

✓ Word-of-mouth advertising can be your best or worst marketing strategy.

✓ Sometimes customers are not aware of all the services your program offers, so tell them.

✓ Some customers know only that they want a safe and caring place to put their child.

UNDERSTANDING YOUR COMPETITORS

Now that you know where your customers are and understand their needs, you need to find out who your competitors are and what they offer to potential customers—as well as the cost for those services. Understanding your competitors helps you design a marketing plan that sets you apart from them. The uniqueness of your program is what will make families choose your organization. Here are some helpful things to know about your competitors:

- What services do they provide?
- What are their hours of operation?
- Do they accept children who are receiving child care subsidies?
- Are their programs ADA accessible? (Do they follow the accessibility guidelines in the Americans with Disabilities Act?)
- Do they offer off-site field trips?
- Do they have family lending libraries?
- What do they charge for their services?
- Do they have a scholarship program for program fees?
- Do they have a multiple-children discount?
- What education do their employees have?
- What are the salary ranges or hourly wages of their employees?
- What is the average length of employment at each competitor?
- Are their programs nationally accredited, or do they participate in the statewide QRIS?

Most likely, more than one organization is competing directly with yours. Locate the programs that offer the same services your program offers, such as other infant-toddler, preschool, school-age, and family child care providers within your geographical area. These programs may be freestanding or may be part of community organizations such as recreation centers or faith-based organizations. Get all your competitors' brochures, check them out online, or make a few phone calls. Once you look at your competitors' marketing materials, you will be able to determine what makes your program different. For instance, let's say your employees have an average tenure of fifteen years, and this is significantly longer than the average length of employment at any of your competitors. If you highlight this fact, it sends a message that your staff is stable and that the children and families can develop consistent relationships with them.

Tips from the Field

✓ Highlight what makes you different from your competitors.

✓ Do your homework; do not assume you know what other programs offer.

✓ Read through other programs' marketing materials to see what information they provide to potential customers.

DEVELOPING A MARKETING PLAN

Now that you know more about your potential customers and competitors, you are ready to create a marketing plan. There is more to a marketing plan than creating a brochure, sending out a one-time mailing, or hosting a booth at the county fair. While a plan can include those things, it must be comprehensive. A marketing plan needs program-specific materials, targeted events, or strategies spread across the calendar year. Spreading your marketing efforts throughout the year divides your time commitment into manageable pieces. Marketing does not have to be expensive, but it should be continual.

How do people get information about child- and youth-serving organizations? Each community is unique, and how individuals get information may vary greatly. Think of the many ways people have found out about your program in the past. If you haven't been collecting that information, add a question to the bottom of your enrollment papers asking, *How did you find out about our program?* This small question will generate a list of marketing avenues. In the meantime, think of places that families frequent, services that families use, and people with whom families come into contact. Here are some avenues that have worked for directors interviewed for this book:

- amusement parks
- community bulletin boards
- community meetings and events
- current staff
- doctors' offices
- libraries
- local colleges and hospitals
- local pools
- local schools
- parent groups
- recreation centers
- social media
- scouting events
- sporting events
- websites
- word-of-mouth

This list offers some suggestions, but it is by no means exhaustive. Take time to create a list that is relevant to your community.

Now it's time to develop a marketing plan. Developing a marketing plan begins with creating materials that communicate your services and that focus on the families who need or want the services you can provide. Let's begin with creating written materials.

Tips from the Field

✓ Doing something is better than doing nothing. Take small steps, and get out there.

✓ Budget for marketing; it takes staff time and materials to make it happen.

✓ Marketing is a great topic for a staff meeting. Including staff in developing a marketing plan and creating marketing materials may produce ideas that you hadn't considered.

CREATING WRITTEN MATERIALS

Written materials come in many forms, such as business cards, newsletters, brochures, event flyers, websites, and more. It is important to have written materials that look professional and that can be easily recognized as materials from your program. The answers to the following questions will help you develop or improve your written marketing materials for potential families:

- Do all your written materials include your program name, logo, and contact information, including your website address?

- Do all your written materials have the same colors, style, and typeface?

- What information are families looking for as they consider purchasing your service? Have you provided that information in your written materials?

- What would make someone pick up your written material and read it?

- Are your written materials translated into the language(s) of families who don't speak English?

Any written materials you present need to be professional. Take time to have all materials proofread for spelling, grammar, punctuation, and typographical errors. Make sure you have a photo release for any person—staff or child—who is pictured in any print or online communication. A release will protect you and allow you to continue to use these materials even after an employee or child leaves your organization.

For potential customers and staff, your written information may be their first exposure to your program. Take time to place written materials at locations where these people might visit, such as colleges, supermarkets, libraries, and coffee shops. Your website may be another place these people will first view your written information. Often potential staff and families will research your organization online prior to an interview, an orientation, or a tour. (For more information on advertising a job opening, please see chapter 10.)

Branding

It is important that your written materials are unique—that they stand out and encourage people to pick them up and read. Branding accomplishes this by helping people easily identify your program. Branding can include a consistent color scheme in all written media, a prominently displayed logo, consistent typeface, and consistent use of terms such as *high-quality* and *family-friendly* that become synonymous with your organization. Put your logo, name, and contact information on everything from your letterhead to your T-shirts. Make sure you have researched and copyrighted your program logo before you send it out into the community or place it online. No matter how great it may look, if it already belongs to someone else, you may cause bad press for your organization or incur a fine for trademark or copyright infringement. Word branding refers to consistent use of words to clearly associate your program with the meaning of those chosen. Word branding should be the same in all written materials. Many programs use children's drawings or photos of children doing an activity. Always get family permission for public display of a child's image or artwork.

Branding also means consistently conveying important information about your program. First and foremost, families want a safe place for their children. They also want their children to enjoy themselves when they are in your program. In your written materials, tell families how your program meets these needs. Include such information as your staff-child ratio, staff education, a short program history, your program's mission and vision, and the types of services you offer (full- or part-time care, half days, extracurricular activities, and so on). If your program is accredited or participates in your state's QRIS, publicize that by using the appropriate accreditation or QRIS logo on your materials. It is always great if you can get some testimonials from current or past families about your organization.

Print Marketing

Print marketing encompasses brochures, newsletters, event flyers, newspaper articles, public service announcements, and direct mail. Your program brochure will likely be the cornerstone of your marketing plan; however, it should not be the only means you use to advertise. Newsletters often go only to the families of children currently attending a program. Sending the newsletter to local community leaders, school secretaries, and families who were interested but did not enroll creates a communication stream with people who can refer families to you, keeping them informed about your program's activities and events. Event flyers or one-page informational flyers about your program should have plenty of white space so they are easy to read and provide pertinent information at a glance.

Child- and youth-serving organizations seldom use newspaper articles and public service announcements, but these can bring great returns. If you decide to pursue this type of marketing, it is important to get guidelines from the local newspaper and cable company so you can learn how to submit articles and announcements. Otherwise, your hard work may end up in the garbage because you did not follow directions. When children in your program do a community service project, you can write a short article—with a photo, if possible—and send it to the local paper. Community-based papers are the easiest to get published in, and they speak to families looking for care within your geographical area. If you are hosting an event such as an open house, you can write both an article and a public service announcement. Send your public service announcement to the local cable company for placement on its public service channel. Ask your employees if they would be interested in taking the lead in documenting and writing short articles when their groups do something noteworthy.

Direct-mail marketing can be more costly than other types of print marketing. But if properly targeted, direct mail can bring great rewards and opportunities to develop relationships with community leaders. For example, one administrator chose ten local companies and called them to find out who did their hiring. Then she sent each hiring manager a packet including a letter of introduction describing the program and its services, several business cards, and the program's brochure. One week later, the administrator contacted each hiring manager. She introduced herself and asked if the manager had any questions. The next group this administrator targeted was pediatricians. This was a great way to introduce the program to community leaders and human resources departments. The administrator figured that if the companies were hiring and the new hires were looking for child care, the companies could suggest her program as an option. She made it easy for them by providing information about the program and linked the information with a name via her follow-up phone call.

Another program director interviewed for this book gave all employees three information packets and asked them to deliver the packets to three community businesses and introduce themselves as employees of the program. The director asked the staff to talk about their program and services and answer any questions businesses might have. The staff received time off for delivering the packets. This strategy provided the companies a face to connect with the program.

When you exhaust your supply of printed materials, it's a good idea to update the materials before reprinting them. Use new pictures, and update the information. Update information at least yearly, so that your print materials are always accurate and current. Unless you are able to print materials in-house, printing costs can be high. So when you're printing brochures, do not print large amounts at a time. It is better to have them reprinted when you need more than to throw away five hundred outdated brochures.

Online Marketing

Next, let's tackle online marketing. Online marketing includes website development and management, social media, and e-mail blasts.

On your website, it's important to duplicate all the information provided in your other written materials. You will also need to maintain the same branding so that your program is recognizable throughout all your written marketing. Use the same color combinations and comments from families and staff about why they chose your program or why they love working there. People often look to comments from others to help them decide whether to choose or buy something. Another key reason to make sure all written information is also on your website is that sometimes your website is the only place people will look for information. Make it user-friendly, inviting, and fun. Some items people like to see on an organization's website include the following:

- clear contact information (phone, e-mail, street address, hours)
- identifiable logo on all pages
- contact form that directs inquiries to the program's e-mail address
- concise information on program mission and vision, staff-child ratios, staff qualifications, and so on

- easy navigation
- forms that can be filled out online (enrollment papers, consent to treat, and so on)
- pricing and subsidy availability
- photos of the environment on all pages
- website visitor counter (visible or invisible)

The biggest mistakes people make when designing a website include the following:

- not routinely updating information
- using too many colors and typefaces (resulting in a busy or chaotic look)
- not using mobile-friendly design
- providing confusing navigation
- using paragraphs instead of bulleted lists

- not using photos (resulting in an impersonal or generic look)
- not providing a way to contact the program online (via website contact form or e-mail)
- using inappropriate or underutilized meta tagging (Meta tags are discussed in greater detail later in this chapter.)

If your program has no website or an inadequate one, you may want a new one but feel that designing it is beyond your ability. That needn't stop you. You may be lucky enough to have an employee in your organization who builds websites. You could hire that staff member to design a website for you at the employee's current hourly rate. You could also contact a local college or vocational school to see if building your website could be a class project. In addition, many organizations offer online tutorials on how to create a website, templates you can use to build your own website, or web design as an additional service. If all else fails, you can hire a freelance webmaster to create your website.

Regardless of how you decide to create your website, you will need to make decisions about its look—color scheme and overall format—before the building begins. You'll also need to have all your materials proofread and in an electronic format ready to be uploaded onto your website. After the website is ready but before it goes live to the public, have several families, employees, and friends review it. Ask them to make sure all the links work and tell you whether the material posted is valuable. Ask them to answer the following questions when they view your website:

- What does the website say to you?
- Is it user-friendly?
- Is the information presented valuable?
- Did the links work?
- Based on the information presented on the website, would you enroll your child in the program?
- Did you find any spelling or grammar errors?
- What kind of device did you use to view the website (PC, Mac, tablet, or smartphone)? Did the website seem to work well on your device?

Having a variety of people review your website will give you many insights into how different people view its design and think about the information on it. This feedback will help you create a website that accurately represents your program and that people will visit.

Your website can be a great marketing tool. But for marketing to succeed, people need to visit your website. There are several ways you can funnel people to your website.

One great way to get families in your community to visit your website is to offer them something they want. Most parents want tips on toilet training, sibling rivalry, biting, and conflict resolution, just to name a few. Pick a few topics that families often struggle with and write an introductory paragraph about the problem followed by a bulleted list of solutions. You can also look for experts in your community and ask them to write short articles on child-related topics, giving the experts credit on your website. These topics could include things like bike safety or sunscreen use. In your newsletter or in an e-mail blast, announce that you have posted a new article on your website. To create a mailing list for e-mail blasts, collect e-mail addresses of past and current families, community leaders, funders, and community newspapers. This low-cost marketing strategy can position your organization as a source of expertise and a place where readers might turn when they need care for their children or youth.

Another way to get visitors to your website—especially relatives and friends of currently enrolled children—is to post children's stories, photos, and artwork.

(Remember that if you are posting images of children or created by children, it's essential to have a release from the family allowing you to do that.) Posting your handbook and allowing families to access it if they have questions helps individuals view your website as a useful resource. As long as you keep updating your website, adding new information, and directing people to your website, they will continue to visit.

Using social media to get the word out about your program's activities and events is a handy, relatively new way to reach current and potential families. Social media does take some time to manage and monitor. The last thing people want to see when they check in with your program on social media is outdated information or that the last post was two months ago. Another reason for constant monitoring is that social media allows commenting by users, and sometimes users post inappropriate or inaccurate information. Simple comments made by staff on social media can have unintended consequences. For instance, let's say an employee posts, "We just got all new computers at the center today. The kids are so excited!" This can tell whoever is paying attention that you have a large amount of new hardware available for the taking. Or suppose another employee comments, "I'm so upset our security system failed yet again. It looks like it is not going to be fixed for at least a week." Now everyone knows your program has zero security. What seems like a simple expression of frustration or excitement can inadvertently provide sensitive information. If your program uses social media, explain to your staff how casual comments can have unintended consequences. This will help them understand why they need to be careful when commenting.

Meta tagging is a method used on websites to help search engines decide which results to display. Search engines such as Google, Bing, and Yahoo! read web pages and, based on the words searched, return what the search engine finds to be the best matches. Meta tags are coding (or programming) statements that describe a web page's content. Search engines use the information you give in a meta tag to help someone searching for that kind of information find your page. The two most important types of meta tags for search engines are keywords meta tags and description meta tags. A keywords meta tag lists the words or phrases that best describe a web page's content. A description meta tag is a one- or two-sentence description of the page.

Your meta tags should be general enough for customers searching broadly yet specific enough for highly focused searchers. At a minimum, your tags should include terms such as *day care, child care, toddler, after-school*, and *center* as well as the name(s) of the street(s) where you are located and the name of your program. It is important to use different spellings and misspellings—for example, use *child care, childcare*, and *chldcre*—so that if a searcher's spelling is off, your site will still come up in the search results. Another key to meta tagging success is making sure your meta tags include anything that is singular about your program. For example, do you have bus service? Other transportation options? Low ratios? Access to a pool? Frequent field trips? Tag everything that makes your program special.

If you are building your website, you can find instructions online or from your website's host or platform about how to place the meta tags within your website's code. If you've hired someone else to build your website, make sure you work with that person to create a list of terms that describe your organization. Not all webmasters will be familiar with your type of service, so do not expect yours to know what tags to use for your website. Meta tagging may seem like a lot of work, but attention to this sort of detail can bring potential customers to your website rather than your competitors' websites.

Tips from the Field

✓ Develop marketing packets to be distributed to local businesses, pediatricians, schools, realtors, and so on to get the word out about your program.

✓ Prepare packets of information before you may need them. Stockpile a few for impromptu tours or visits to your program.

✓ Maximize your presence on the Internet.

✓ Do not forget social media when thinking of quick and easy marketing tools.

COMMUNITY INVOLVEMENT

Being involved within your community can also be a great marketing strategy. If you do not participate in community events or meetings, chances are good that many community members do not know of your program or what it offers. An entire group of potential customers or marketers may have no idea of your existence.

Community involvement can serve your program well. Attending meetings can give you information about resources and services that might benefit your families and your program, such as family-friendly events held in the community, utility payment assistance programs, free medical screening, and adult continuing education programs. In addition, these meetings can provide an appropriate avenue to discuss your program and provide participants with a take-home flyer for future reference. Often, at these meetings, you will meet the movers and shakers within your community. These people will be more willing to give information about upcoming events and resources to someone they've met than someone they've never met.

It is important to make sure that your community involvement is a good fit for your program. Attend community meetings that are related to the service you offer. For example, it would be more appropriate for you to align with your county's jobs and family services department, a local foundation, or a state licensing review committee than with the city planning commission. While the city planning commission may have a high profile and include many influential individuals, engaging with the jobs and family services department will provide you with a connection for receiving prompt updates and procedural changes that affect how you do your job. Local foundations, for their part, can give you information about funding resources. And volunteering for a licensing review committee can give you some say in the core knowledge that staff need to have to work with children. Each group, in its own way, can benefit your program's operation and funding. Your time to attend community meetings may be limited, so choose wisely. Do your research. Look at new initiatives that will affect child- and youth-serving programs. There may be many to choose from, so taking your time and doing your research will help you find a good fit right from the start.

When you participate in community events or attend community meetings, bring marketing materials to pass out. Alternatively, you could create an event and invite your fellow members of community groups to attend.

Tips from the Field

✓ It is easy to get trapped in your own little world. For the sake of your program's vitality, you need to connect with other community leaders.

✓ Create collaborative agreements with community organizations to provide such things as volunteers or use of buildings or sports facilities.

✓ Communicating with community leaders and participating in community meetings are important, but you need to strike a balance. It is easy to get overinvolved, so target your efforts carefully.

✓ Identify what community engagement looks like in your community. Identify a resource within the community with whom you can develop a mutually supportive relationship.

✓ When you attend a community meeting, bring information about your program, even if it is just the latest newsletter. Make sure to bring something different each time, so people won't look at your material, say they already have that, and walk away.

✓ Look at the agendas of community meetings. Is there anything you've done that dovetails with an agenda item? For instance, perhaps the local chamber of commerce is looking for children's artwork to hang in its office or is sponsoring a family day and needs a few developmentally appropriate activities for preschoolers. Offer what you have. If it is used, display a sign saying, "Preschool activities (or artwork) provided by (your program name)."

WHY MARKETING IS IMPORTANT

Many programs are full all the time, and their directors may feel that marketing is not necessary. These programs may be full because their directors are already doing the things listed in this chapter and never considered these strategies to be marketing. Other directors may feel that marketing is a waste of time and money. They think that they do not have enough money or time for marketing, so they simply don't do it.

Not marketing themselves is one of the biggest mistakes organizations can make. Marketing is crucial to a positive public image, financial security, and ongoing program success. Even if your program is full, enrollment and staff will fluctuate, and your current families will eventually outgrow your services. To fill empty spots quickly, you will need to market your program so you can generate a pool of additional clients. This is doubly true if you are considering expanding. Marketing can not only provide you with clients but also create community partnerships that bring in additional services and dollars.

Marketing should be intentional and ongoing. That is not to say you should do every marketing task every week. Determine the marketing strategies that you would like to use, and then look at your calendar and set aside time to get them done as part of your regular job duties. Rather than take on the entire world at once, start small. For instance, during your first month on the job, you can review and update all written materials and make sure they are in an electronic format so they are easy to access, update, and print when needed. Develop the habit of taking marketing materials with you everywhere.

Above all, marketing is about getting people in the door. Your program may be great, but if no one knocks on the door, you will still have spots to fill. You can do many things to attract people to visit your program. For example, host an event such as an open house, create an event such as an art fair, or have the children in your program put on a play, and invite family members and community leaders to see it. When you attend a community event such as a county fair, display pictures of program events and field trips, or play a video that showcases your staff, families, and environment. Loop the video so it plays continuously while you are at the event. Such videos are also great to show at open houses and program events held in your own facility. You might even show this type of video at staff orientations or interviews to give candidates a view of your program. Remember to obtain photo releases for the individuals in the photos and site releases for photos that show sites other than your own (such as field trip photos).

This section's Tips from the Field recaps some of the low-cost and no-cost marketing ideas in this chapter and adds a few more for your consideration.

Tips from the Field

- ✓ Visit local businesses and introduce yourself and your program.

- ✓ Write articles for your community's newspaper.

- ✓ Create an e-mail distribution list, and use it to send e-mail blasts about program information and events.

- ✓ Maximize your online presence by keeping your website up to date, using meta tags, and using social media.

- ✓ Offer a referral stipend to any family who refers another family to the program.

- ✓ Post program information on local community information boards.

- ✓ Partner with organizations that serve the same clientele, such as a dance or martial arts studio, to publicize one another mutually.

- ✓ Host tours and open houses to get people in the door so they can see what you are all about.

Balancing Work and Home

When your work life and personal life are out of balance, your stress level is likely to soar.

MAYO CLINIC, MAYOCLINIC.ORG

You are sitting in the administrator's chair now, with so much to do that you are spending more and more time at work. Worse yet, you are taking work home. Your family is complaining that you are never home, and even when you are home, you are working. The harsh reality of your job is that there will always be more things to do. You may feel less like an administrator than a firefighter putting out fires all day long. So how can you lower your stress level? How do you set boundaries and create a balance between work and home?

PLANNING YOUR DAY

First, you need to know one important thing about yourself: Are you a morning or evening person? The majority of your work hours should reflect that preference. If you are a morning person, come in before your operating hours to get things done and to plan your day without interruptions. If you work best at night, stay after hours to tie up loose ends and to set a plan for tomorrow's work.

Whichever sort of person you are, it is important to balance your work time so that you can see both ends of the day and be available to families both in the morning and in the afternoon. Beginning your day in quiet can help you look at your workload accurately and determine what you can complete realistically. You can also use this time to complete tasks that need concentration and no distractions. Ending your day in quiet can help you finish up tasks, and it allows you to decompress and reflect on the next day's events, as well as complete tasks that require your undivided attention. Whether you make each day's plan that morning or the preceding afternoon, beginning the day with a plan helps you be proactive rather than reactive. While you cannot foresee all issues that might arise in a given day, having processes and procedures for every-day events will minimize the fires you need to put out each day.

It is easy to let your job consume all your time. To prevent this, begin by setting your work hours—and when the end of your day comes, go home. If you feel you cannot leave your staff in charge while you attend a meeting or have a day off, then you have some work to do to prepare your staff for leadership when you are not there. For many organizations, it is financially impossible to have an assistant administrator. If that is your situation, identify an employee who can lead in your stead if you are unavailable. One director interviewed for this book designed a how-to binder outlining how program-related processes and issues had been addressed in the past. This binder helped staff act independently and confidently when the director was out of the building. While it is hard to foresee all the times you will need to leave the building, it is important to create a sched-ule that states clearly when you typically will be in the building. Communicate that schedule to families and staff. This schedule will help them trust that you will be available at specific times if they need your assistance or advice.

Tips from the Field

✓ You need to set aside time for admin-istrative work. It's okay to close the door so you can complete your work without interruption.

✓ Look for volunteers who could help you with clerical tasks.

✓ Develop boundaries after 6:00 p.m. The evening is your time to dedicate to family and friends.

✓ Make a daily plan, and then follow the plan.

✓ Do not read any e-mails on the weekend. That is family time.

KEEPING WORK AT WORK

You have probably already discovered that you could work 24–7 and still not com-plete everything that needs to be done in a given day. In a society full of phones capable of delivering calls, texts, e-mails, and social media almost anywhere, at any hour, and full of people wanting immediate response and gratification, it can be hard to leave work at work. But bringing work home or working longer hours at work does not necessarily mean that more things are getting done efficiently or accurately. James Surowiecki (2014) states in his *New Yorker* article "The Cult of Overwork" that as "we've known for a while, long hours diminish both productivity and quality."

One key to success as an administrator is keeping your work at work. At times you will need to come in early or work late, but these times should be the exception, not the rule. It is important to set work hours that support staff and families while providing you time to recharge with family and friends. In an article titled "Work-Life Balance: Tips to Reclaim Control," the Mayo Clinic (2015) outlines the costs of being married to your work: fatigue, poor health, lost time with family and loved ones, and increased expectations to complete additional work.

Most administrators struggle with being all things to all people and often feel disloyal to staff and families when they take time off. Remember to give yourself permission to take care of you. If you begin to feel that your program, with all its ups and downs, is interfering with your family life, your attitude will become negative. You may lose your passion for your work and eventually leave the field. It is okay to take an occasional day off to clean your house, go shopping, read a good book, or just veg out. These are all things that allow people to relax and let go of the many stresses that come from work.

Tips from the Field

✓ Create a balanced life that includes work, leisure, and positive relationships. All three are equally important.

✓ Time with family and friends can renew your energy to help you meet the challenges of the next workday.

✓ If you have an idea for work outside of your work hours, write it down so you do not forget it, and then go back to your family and friends.

✓ After business hours and when you are not on call, turn off your phone or lower the volume so you are not tempted to answer each beep.

✓ Remember: vacation is vacation. If you've trained your staff well enough, all will be fine until you get back.

COPING WITH STRESS

Stress is often caused by a major life event, such as a new baby, moving, the death of a loved one, or changing jobs. Here you are in a new job with so many new things to learn and potentially not too many people to lean on. No stress there, right? You may feel pulled in so many directions that it may be hard to keep yourself on track. Add work stress to family stress, and now you are not just off track but blasting into orbit. Stress can cause you to be short with people, make decisions in the heat of the moment, or just shut down altogether.

It is important to develop some relaxation strategies to help you cope with stress. Using stress-reduction techniques can help you shake off the sense of being overworked or unable to deal with a disgruntled parent or a demanding employee, allowing you to regain focus and keep moving forward constructively. While it would be great to take the next plane to a sunny beach, that is not always possible. So let's look at a few quick techniques that could help you let go and move on:

- Take a walk outside for ten minutes.

- Put on your tennis shoes, and run a mile.

- Close your office door, then close your eyes for ten minutes, and do not answer the phone. Using a warm compress on the back of your neck can also be helpful.

- Breathe in through your nose to the count of ten, and breathe out of your mouth to the count of ten. Repeat ten times.

- Meditate for five minutes, and continually repeat, "I am a good person."

- Call a friend who might be able to give you a different take on the situation.

- Envision yourself at your favorite place. Think about the sounds, the smells, the climate, and the colors, and begin to relax.

- Beginning at the top of your head, tense your muscles, and then relax the muscles. Proceed down your body until you've tensed and relaxed your toes.

Each of these techniques should take no more than fifteen minutes. Not all techniques work for all people, so find the ones that work for you. Choosing an ongoing stress reliever can also be very helpful. Some popular stress-relieving techniques, such as an exercise routine, yoga, or tai chi, can be very beneficial when done regularly. Scheduling regular opportunities to relax is healthy for your mind and your body. When you feel good about yourself, it is easier to deal with each day's challenges. When all else fails, a good laugh can ease a lot of stress in short order.

Tips from the Field

✔ Taking care of yourself is the best gift you can give to your program.

✔ It is okay not to know all the answers.

✔ Everyone deserves a smile and respect, regardless of how the person is treating you.

✔ If you are dealing with disgruntled family members, acknowledge where they are coming from.

✔ Remember that you are not the only one who has stress in your life. Remember how you would like to be treated, and treat others the same way.

PART 2

Down to the Nitty-Gritty

The next two chapters of this book will help you get a handle on the nitty-gritty of expenses and revenue. These tasks may seem daunting. You have so many other things to do. And meanwhile, staff and families want you to solve all their problems. But your program's finances are a crucial aspect of your job. The only way to get started on this duty is to take the first step. Taking time to understand both the expenditure and income sides of the budget can prevent major financial issues later.

Budgeting

Watch the costs and the profits will take care of themselves.

ANDREW CARNEGIE, "AMERICAN EXPERIENCE: ANDREW CARNEGIE"

In some situations you are given a budget, and in others, you need to create one. Budgets allocate money for specific items or purposes. Understanding the types of budgets and the purpose of each type of budget is a good first step in getting a handle on your program's finances.

TYPES OF BUDGETS

Large organizations typically use a master budget. This is a comprehensive budget that combines the income and expenditures for all aspects or departments of the organization. From this master budget, individual department or program budgets are created so the cost for such things as building maintenance, building rent or lease, heat, administration, and so on can be split among all the organization's departments. Often each part of the organization, such as each site in a multisite program, is considered a cost center within the larger budget. This type of traditional budget looks at the past few years' expenditures and forecasts the next fiscal year's spending in each area. It incorporates cost-of-living increases for materials, supplies, and staff. A new organization that has no history upon which to base projections should keep records of all expenditures, not only for creating subsequent budgets but also for tax purposes.

The most common type of budget is an organizational budget. Small organizations and departments of larger organizations typically use this type of budget because it focuses on day-to-day expenditures and revenues. This allows the budget to be broken down into small increments and allows an administrator to adjust the budget to meet the ebbs and flows of expenditures and revenues. For a detailed discussion of understanding expenditures, see the next section in this chapter. For more on understanding revenue, see chapter 9.

The type of budget you use will depend on a few variables, such as the scope of services provided by the parent organization, the number of locations of service, and the diversity of the income streams. If your program is part of a larger organization, have a meeting with the person who creates the budgets to understand how this person determined the dollars allotted for each item within your program budget. Regardless of the type of budget you use, remember that budgeting and monitoring of budgets take time. It is important to plan time to review your budget weekly. A great way to minimize tracking time is to use software that allows you to input your revenues and expenditures as they occur. Once you've entered the receipts for expenditures and revenues, you can generate a report that tells you how you are doing on each line item. To determine what software to use, talk to your organization's certified public accountant (CPA) or the person who develops your organizational budget. Use the same software to track your budget as is used to create it. This will save you time, because you will be able to upload program information quickly into the master system.

Tips from the Field

✓ Get a mentor to help you understand the type of budget your organization uses and your role in developing the budget.

✓ If you did not create your budget, take time to understand both the revenue and expenditure sides and how the dollars allocated in each line item were determined.

✓ If you create your own budget, be able to explain each line item and justify the amount budgeted in each line item.

✓ Choose a management company to handle the more difficult and time-sensitive financial issues related to your organization's operation.

If you are creating your own budget, choosing the type of budget is a first step. Meeting with the CPA who will be doing your taxes to determine what software to use will help you provide information in the same format, eliminating redundancy. It is also important for you to understand accounting terminology. For example, your accountant may ask for a P&L report for your department. The abbreviation *P&L* stands for "profit and loss." This report can be generated from most accounting software. It outlines the expenditures and revenues by cost centers for a specific period of time—usually quarterly or yearly. In addition, this report can compare your current income and expenses to those of the previous year. This comparison can give you a clear indication of which way you are heading (into the red or into the black). Many websites define accounting terms and give you the abbreviations for these terms. Using your search engine, type "accounting terms" in the search bar, and you will find many sites to choose from.

UNDERSTANDING EXPENDITURES

Expenditures are all the things that require you to set aside dollars so that you can disburse funds to a second party. When you're creating a budget, you list all expenditures of each type under a line item, such as "staff costs" or "building costs." To label expenses efficiently, give each line item a number, often referred to as a "cost code." For instance, if you code staff costs as 1200, then the subcosts within that line item (the subitems) would have subcodes such as 1201 for salary, 1202 for workers' compensation, and so on. This signals that anything coded with a 1200 number belongs to staff costs. It also allows an administrator to look at each line item and track spending in each subitem as well as the overall line item. This type of coding gives a running account of expenditures and allows close monitoring of each area in the budget.

You can find a sample program budget in appendix D. In this chapter and in the sample budget, the expenditures discussed are some of the most common line items and subitems for child- and youth-serving organizations. They are by no means an exhaustive list and are just meant to provide examples to show you how to construct a budget based on your expenditures. Depending on your specific situation, you may wish to add or delete line items or subitems. In the following sections, let's take a look at some common line items and some costs within those line items.

Tips from the Field

✓ Label all receipts with the appropriate cost codes at the time of purchase.

✓ Create one place to put all your receipts.

✓ Plan time weekly to enter all expenditures and revenues into your accounting software.

✓ If you do not understand a term or process, ask about it.

✓ Meet with your CPA quarterly so you can fix any problems in a timely manner.

STAFFING COSTS

Staffing your organization is likely the biggest expenditure you will encounter as a director. The makeup of a child- or youth-serving program's staff can be very diverse. It may comprise several different types of staff, such as clerical, administrative, frontline, and food-service employees. Once you have determined the amount and scope of staff you need (see "Your Staffing Needs" in chapter 10), it is important to visit the US Department of Labor (DOL) website at www.dol.gov. Here you can find the latest information on labor legislation. Review the rules that define an exempt employee (a status that limits the payment of overtime), and review how the amount of hours worked by an employee can determine what, if any, health-care benefits the employer must offer the employee. The DOL provides many fact sheets that help you determine how your staff should be classified and what you will need to budget for staff.

Staff expenditures may include some or all of the following:

- salary
- federal, state, and local taxes
- social security
- workers' compensation
- benefits
- staff incentives
- background checks
- professional organization membership dues
- orientation
- professional development
- substitutes

When you begin thinking about staff costs, you might initially think only of the hourly rate paid to employees. However, staff costs include much more. For instance, you must withhold federal, state, and local income taxes; social security; and Medicare from each employee's salary and submit the appropriate amount to the correct agency at the correct time. Money for workers' compensation premiums is another cost directly related to employees, so it should be included under the staffing costs line item. The rate charged for workers' compensation premiums depends on how your program is classified. Classification is based on the overall business conducted by the organization. For programs affiliated with the federal government, it is best to check with the DOL for classification. Workers' compensation for private organizations is administered through each state's bureau of workers' compensation. On your state bureau's website, you will be able to determine your classification and the policy premiums assigned to that classification. This website may also provide applications, claim information, and the ability to pay premiums online. In addition to taxes and workers' compensation expenses, you also need to include any benefits you provide, such as an individual retirement account (IRA) match, a shared cost in health insurance, or paying the entire cost for life insurance. Most state licensing agencies require staff background checks, and the cost for these should be listed as staffing costs. The costs of interviewing, conducting orientation, completing paperwork, and coaching new employees are often overlooked. These tasks are directly related to hiring and orienting staff to the program and therefore belong in the staffing costs line item.

This part of your budget is also a great place to set aside money for staff incentives, such as food for staff meetings, gift cards on employees' work anniversaries or birthdays, and holiday gifts or year-end bonuses. Not all programs have funds for major staff incentives, but even small sums to provide snacks for the break room or cards for birthdays can go a long way to establish staff satisfaction. Please see chapter 13 for more staff retention ideas.

It's easy to overlook professional development costs, but it is important to budget for these. Ongoing education of staff is essential to providing high-quality programming. Many state licensing agencies, QRIS programs, and national accrediting organizations require ongoing professional development. You may encounter some disagreement as to what costs associated with ongoing professional development, other than the cost of training, should be paid by your program. According to the DOL Wage and Hour Division's "Fact Sheet #46: Daycare Centers and Preschools under the Fair Labor Standards Act (FLSA)," "The time spent attending training that is required by the state for day care center licensing is working time for which employees must be compensated" (DOL 2009). For this reason, not only the cost of training but also staff salaries for the training hours paid in addition to employees' regularly paid hours should be included in the staffing costs line item. Some organizations will also pay the employee a meal stipend if meals are not provided at the training. Still others will pay any fee associated with receiving a certification that is directly related to the employee's job. Finally, include in this line item all costs for outside substitutes who are not already part of your permanent staff.

Now that you know what goes into the staffing costs line item, how do you determine how many staff you need for the number of children you have, so you can determine what your salary costs will be? To figure this out, you will need to know several things: your average enrollment for each classroom, the required adult-child ratio per class, your maximum group size per class, and your daily hours of operation. In addition, you will need to know what constitutes a full-time equivalent (FTE) in your organization. An FTE is whatever equates to one person working full-time, as determined by your organization. With this information, you will be able to calculate how many staff you need to operate your program. Aim to calculate the total hours for a makeup of 70 percent full-time and 30 percent part-time employees to be able to cover vacations, sick days, lunches, and breaks. Following is an example showing how one program's staffing works.

Program A operates twelve hours a day. Full-time employees work forty hours per week in five eight-hour shifts. The following table provides the data needed to determine how many FTEs and part-time staff Program A needs to maintain the proper adult-child ratios and group sizes.

Room type	Number of rooms	Adult:child ratio	Maximum group size	Average attendance	Number of staff needed to maintain ratio and group size	Daily hours of operation	Daily staff hours needed (number of staff needed multiplied by daily hours of operation)
Infant	2	1:3	12	12	8	12	**96**
Toddler	2	1:6	12	12	4	12	**48**
Preschool	2	1:12	12	12	2	12	**24**
School-age	1	1:18	36	36	2	6	**12**
							180 (total)

Next, Program A's director multiplies 180 hours per day by 5 days per week to find that the program needs 900 staff hours per week. From there, the director can determine how many full-time and part-time employees the program needs, using a mix of 70 percent full-time and 30 percent part-time staff.

900	Staff hours needed per week to maintain Program A's ratios and maximum group sizes
× 52	Multiply weekly staff hours needed by the number of weeks in the year.
= 46,800	**Staff hours needed per year**
÷ 2080	Divide yearly staff hours by 2080 hours, which is the number of hours a full-time employee (40 hours a week) works in 1 year. Round to nearest whole number.
= 23	**Full-time workers needed**
× 0.70	Multiply 23 by 0.70 to determine how many full-time employees are needed if 70% of staff work full-time. Round to nearest whole number.
= 16	**Full-time employees needed at 70% full-time staffing**
23 − 16	Subtract 16 from 23 to determine how many part-time employees are needed if 30% of staff work part-time.
= 7	**Part-time employees needed at 30% part-time staffing**

These calculations determine only the amount of staff Program A needs to cover its classrooms. The calculations do not account for administrative, secretarial, janitorial, kitchen, or accounting services.

When a program operates from 6:00 a.m. to 6:00 p.m. each day, that equals twelve daily operation hours. If employees work eight-hour shifts, the program will need staff for the remaining four hours of each day. Often, part-time staff or those who work before- and after-care programs work only five or six hours per day; they can achieve an eight-hour day by filling in for breaks, lunches, staff training, community meetings, staff mentoring, lesson planning time, and so forth.

Tips from the Field

✓ You can minimize staffing costs by using college students who need practicum and work-study hours.

✓ Apply for an AmeriCorps VISTA worker who stays with your program for a year. VISTA workers focus their efforts on building the organizational, administrative, and financial capacity of organizations that fight illiteracy, improve health services, foster economic development, and otherwise assist low-income communities. VISTA workers develop programs to meet a need, write grants, and recruit and train volunteers and can do a variety of administrative duties, such as marketing and events planning.

Nonprofit organizations, schools, community groups, faith-based groups, and public agencies located in low-income urban and rural areas can apply to sponsor a VISTA worker. For more information, visit www.nationalservice.gov /programs/americorps-programs /americorps-vista/sponsor-vista -project.

✓ If your state allows the use of high school students or students in a child care vocational certification setting to serve as classroom aides, it is a great way to provide additional staff at a reduced cost.

BUILDING COSTS

Building costs, like staffing costs, have the potential to add up unexpectedly. This is especially likely if when you develop a budget, you do not consider the following expenses:

- mortgage or rent
- utilities
- security
- maintenance
- cleaning services
- lawn care
- snow removal
- inspection fees

Building costs vary from organization to organization. A lot depends on whether you are purchasing or renting your program space. Mortgage or rent is a fixed, predictable cost, but other building costs can be hard to predict. For example, the costs of utilities such as gas, electricity, and water are based on your usage. Usage often fluctuates with the weather; extreme temperatures can raise costs. Since weather is hard to predict, your best bet is to look at the total yearly cost for each utility over the past two years, take the largest number, and add 20 percent to create an inflation buffer.

Remember to include in your building costs any expenses for security items. These may include exterior and interior surveillance cameras, equipment to record the surveillance, and external data storage. These costs could also include installing exterior lighting fixtures, an intercom system for the main entry door, or a monthly monitoring fee by a security company.

Your ongoing maintenance costs will depend on whether you are renting the program space or purchasing the property. If you are renting the property, read your lease to determine what maintenance the property owner has agreed to pay for and what will be your responsibility. If you own or are purchasing a building, all maintenance costs are your responsibility.

Once you understand your responsibility, determine who has performed any maintenance on your building and the cost of that maintenance for the past two years. Introduce yourself to those individuals or companies. Some organizations use a property management company, and others hire an independent maintenance person. Research each approach before something needs to be fixed. Knowing who is bonded and who has insurance now will be very important if something does not go as planned later. In addition, you will need to determine the typical wait time for each type of maintenance company. For instance, a large company may have more workers than an independent contractor, but that does not mean the company will be Johnny-on-the-spot. A large company may be less customer-friendly because it has so many customers. Check references, and then trust your own intuition. Remember that you can always change your mind if companies or contractors do not hold up their end of the bargain. Understand the various services offered and the estimated cost for each. If you take time to educate yourself prior to a needed repair, you will not have to settle for whoever can do the repair regardless of the cost.

Each facility comes with a specific set of mechanicals. Mechanicals are devices that support the efficient workings of a building. They include the following:

- heating units
- air-conditioning units
- water heaters
- electrical systems
- plumbing
- roof, gutters, and downspouts

It is important to know how old each of these mechanicals is and when it was last serviced. The older it is, the more likely it is to need replacing and to need more dollars allocated within the budget. As you forecast when something will need to be replaced, place money for that replacement in the line item for capital improvements. A capital improvement is the replacement or remodeling of some aspect of a property that will enhance the property's value and will last longer than one calendar year. This strategy can create an unencumbered fund you can use whenever a major repair or replacement needs to be done. An unencumbered fund is a reserve that is set aside for a specific purpose. When you create your budget, it is helpful to provide a different subitem for each such replacement or remodel within the capital improvements line item. This will allow you to monitor the funds for each project. For more information on long-term capital projects, see the section devoted to this topic later in this chapter. Note: if you are considering purchasing a program space, it is important to have an independent building inspector check each of the mechanicals and give you an unbiased opinion as to when they will need to be repaired or replaced.

Some programs use donated space, so those programs do not pay mortgage or rent. However, no contract—donation, lease, or mortgage—would cover all items required to run the program efficiently. Even small items, like the paper towels and disinfectant spray used to clean tables, can cost a significant amount over the course of a budget cycle. Understand what costs you bear in caring for your space. Cleaning, lawn care, and snow removal costs are often forgotten in the building costs line item of a budget. Sometimes the work itself is delegated to staff as part of their job description. Some research on your part is in order. Determine whom your program has used in the past, what was included in their services, and the costs for those services. Find out when each service is up for renewal. Allow yourself ample time to renegotiate current contracts or find a new supplier. Some property management companies include these services, but others don't; you will need to know for sure so you can budget correctly. If you use a property management company, check to see if the cleaning, lawn care, and snow removal supplies are included in your service contract. Determine if services provided by existing contractors have been sufficient or if it is time for a change or a contract renegotiation. If you decide to remain with existing contractors, make sure you know whether your payments will increase. If cleaning, lawn care, or snow removal becomes the responsibility of a staff member, remember that the employee will need the proper supplies. For example, an employee responsible for cleaning will need cleaning solutions, brooms, mops, a vacuum, paper towels, toilet paper, and so on. Once you have determined all your costs for cleaning, lawn care, and snow removal services, supplies, and equipment, you can plug them into your budget.

Inspection fees are something many programs do not budget for. Inspections for things such as fire extinguishers, septic systems, building codes, and health codes are not free. Usually the yearly fees are posted on inspection agency websites; if not, call and ask about fees. Do not assume there are no fees for services rendered just because they are not listed on the website. Also, remember that some inspections happen more than yearly, and budget accordingly.

Tips from the Field

✓ Create a calendar that indicates when all service contracts are up for renewal, with a reminder two months prior to allow for renegotiation or to request bids for those services.

✓ Most failures of building equipment are caused by lack of routine maintenance. Routine maintenance builds in facility reliability.

✓ Read all your building-related contracts. If a contract does not say something is included, it is not included.

EQUIPMENT COSTS

Child- and youth-serving organizations have plenty of equipment, and equipment does not last forever. It can also need maintenance, so it's wise to place money for that in your budget's equipment costs line item. Equipment costs include the following:

- computers
- Internet
- landline and mobile phones
- copiers and printers
- refrigeration units

In an age when everything can be found or bought online and children's schoolwork and learning software is online, child- and youth-serving programs need computers within the program as well as in the administrator's office. The speed at which computer hardware and software becomes obsolete is mind-boggling. Not only do you need to allocate money for the computers, tablets, computer tables, software (applications), and any other computer-related equipment your program needs, you also need to make sure that you set money aside for updating this equipment. Buying these items may not be a yearly event, but the need to repair or replace them in case of viruses or physical damage can be unpredictable. Costs for Internet services can be as varied as the number of providers within your area. You will need Internet access to buy items, pay bills, access your bank, file reports, communicate with families, market your program, enhance learning opportunities for children and staff, and much more. Remember to include in this line subitem software costs for accounting programs, security software, menu creation software, and so forth.

Telephone costs can take several forms. Some programs use only mobile phones. Others use only landlines. Still others use a combination of the two. Whichever configuration you use, to run your business, families must be able to reach you. Most state licensing agencies require a child- or youth-serving organization to have a phone number that is dedicated to the program. In some states a landline is required to be housed within the program space. Other states allow the use of a mobile phone as the point of contact for the program. Check with your licensing agency to determine the specific criteria for the type and use of a telephone within your program. In addition to a program phone, some programs have phones to communicate between rooms, with the administrator's office, and with the world outside the program space. Other programs use mobile phones for these purposes and for field trips. It is common for employees to have personal mobile phones. But it will be up to your organization to determine whether staff may carry their personal phones while working and whether they're expected to use their personal phones for work-related calls. It's also up to the organization to determine whether to pay part or all of the phone bill for use of a personal mobile phone during work hours. Telephone costs should include any and all charges for phone services, including data plans if required, as well as mobile phone insurance or a replacement policy.

With costs for copiers and printers going down, some organizations have begun purchasing smaller desktop all-in-one machines that can not only print but also scan, fax, and make copies. For these machines, there is a one-time cost for purchase and an additional cost for toner and paper, which is discussed under office supplies in the next section. Usually the costs to repair these units are equal to or greater than buying a new unit. If your machine will no longer be under warranty this year, it's important to put money into this line item in case you need a replacement. Programs that do a large amount of printing or copying each month may opt to lease a copier. With a copier lease comes a maintenance agreement that pays for a defined amount of service calls and a specific amount of copies. There is an additional charge for copies over the prescribed amount. Toner and paper costs for leased machines are typically the responsibility of the program. Look at last year's budget to determine how much money was allocated for this subitem, and add 20 percent to cover any additional costs.

All child- and youth-serving organizations have refrigeration units. If you have a full-service kitchen, see the discussion on refrigeration in the section on program material costs. If you do not have a full-service kitchen, put refrigeration costs here. Costs within this line subitem may fluctuate from year to year. If your unit was just purchased and is still under warranty, you might allocate a small amount here. However, if the unit is eight years old, you might allocate replacement cost here or in the capital projects line item.

OFFICE SUPPLY COSTS

Office supplies are simply a part of doing business. Here are some common costs under this budget line item:

- paper
- toner
- postage
- credit card processing fees
- marketing materials

Paper and toner are a major expense in this area. Toner companies will deliver toner directly to you at specified times, such as monthly. If you use a toner company, place toner costs and service fees in this line item. Purchasing paper by the case is the most cost-effective approach. Look at last year's consumption, and use it as a guide for deciding what to allocate this year.

To handle their postage needs, some programs simply purchase rolls of stamps. Others keep a postage meter provided by the post office and have postage loaded into the meter whenever it is needed. Still other programs purchase their postage online. Regardless of how you purchase postage, you can determine an amount to budget by reviewing last year's budget.

If your organization accepts credit and debit cards for program payments, include in your office supply costs the fees credit card companies and banks charge for processing card payments. These fees can add up substantially over the course of a year. To determine the total figure, look at the cost charged per transaction, and multiply that by the number of families who use a credit or debit card. Multiply that figure by fifty-two if families pay weekly or by twelve if families pay monthly. Even though the number of families using a credit or debit card may change over the course of a year, this strategy will give you a reasonable figure to allocate for the payment-processing line subitem.

Items used for marketing your organization belong in the office supplies line item, too. This includes the costs of such things as business cards, letterhead, program brochures, newsletters, and advertisements. Some organizations place costs associated with family events, such as family nights out, family dinners, and holiday nights out, within the marketing subitem because these events showcase their program and therefore are a type of marketing. Creating a specific line subitem so you can track marketing spending and compare it to enrollment will help you assess the effectiveness of your marketing efforts.

One item in the budget that is often forgotten is banking fees. Fees for checks and checking accounts can be a surprise if you have never balanced a checking account before and are unaware of these costs. Some banks charge a monthly fee, while others offer free checking if you make a certain dollar amount of deposits per month. Have a conversation with your bank to determine what services you need and the fees associated with each service. Once you know what the fees are, make sure you record them accurately in the appropriate line item of your budget. It is always good to shop around for banking services; they will be as diverse as the banking opportunities in your area. Knowing this information will prevent you from finding an expenditure that does not have a line item and has no money allocated.

The miscellaneous category of office supply costs is where you can list the costs of various other items that you use within the office. As the person who develops the budget, you can decide what belongs in this line subitem. Be sure to define what will go in this category so you can tabulate like items appropriately. Some things that you might list in this category are pens, pencils, notepads, receipt books, program decorations, envelopes, file folders, and so on. Some people include the tracking of their petty cash in this area. This provides an idea of how much money has been spent and whether more money needs to be transferred to this line item to cover costs associated with petty cash. This category can be very broad. It may include items that are used only once a year or do not seem to fit anywhere else.

Tips from the Field

✓ It is important to monitor petty cash closely, if not daily, as it is the budget area most likely to be misused or abused.

✓ Create a petty cash voucher on which employees must write the name of the place where an item has been purchased (the vendor), who purchased the item, the cost of the item, where this cost belongs in the budget, and a signature and date. Staple the receipt for the item purchased to the voucher. See appendix E for a sample petty cash voucher.

✓ Number your petty cash vouchers so you can tell if you are missing a purchase documentation.

✓ If a mistake has been made on a petty cash voucher, void it, and place it back in the box so you know that you are not missing a purchase.

✓ You can provide a reduced fee to families who pay cash to reduce your program's credit card processing fee expenditure.

✓ Buying office supplies in bulk can significantly reduce the overall cost.

✓ Getting a rewards card from your office supplier can provide you with coupons and additional discounts for frequently used supplies.

✓ Using a company that routinely ships toner can reduce the cost of each unit and make sure you do not run out.

✓ Determine if any of your parents or staff members work in or know someone who works in a print shop to print your marketing materials; this might reduce your overall cost.

✓ Always negotiate your printing costs and balance the volume printed with the estimated usage. Do not overprint just to get a lower price.

PROGRAM MATERIAL COSTS

Program materials used within your program space vary depending on the activity that takes place within each room. For instance, a large-motor room might include mats and climbing equipment, and a program space where free time occurs might contain other items. For budgeting purposes, program materials such as the following are defined as permanent fixtures:

- chairs
- cribs
- crib mattresses
- high chairs
- storage cabinets
- shelving
- sensory tables
- tables

While permanent fixtures are usually purchased when the program first opens, things will need to be replaced periodically. For example, let's say the numbers of children enrolled in certain age groups of your program fluctuate, and you find yourself with more preschoolers than infants or more school-agers than toddlers. Suddenly you need more tables and chairs for preschoolers or school-agers. As you determine the dollar amount to allocate in your budget for your program materials line item, you may want to look at all your permanent fixtures to see if any should be replaced or updated to accommodate your current enrollment.

If you have a full-service kitchen and cook meals and snacks in-house, purchase prepackaged snacks, or contract to have all meals cooked and served, you will need a food service subitem under your program materials line item. Here are some of the things this subitem could include:

- refrigerators
- stoves or ovens
- microwaves
- dishwashers
- food service contract
- food
- consumable supplies

Even if you contract for food service or have children bring food from home, your program probably has a refrigerator and microwave for storing and heating food. If you have a full-service kitchen, then you may also have a stove and dishwasher. These are all major appliances. If they're not under warranty, you may need to allocate money for appliance service calls.

This line subitem is also where you should budget for contracted food service. If you are on the US Department of Agriculture (USDA) Child and Adult Care Food Program (CACFP), make sure your food service contractor is aware of the list of creditable foods and portion sizes. If you need to supplement foods to comply with CACFP guidelines, then you should budget for that food in this category. For more information on the benefits of participating in CACFP, see the section on this topic in chapter 9. The subitem listed as "food" in the sample budget (appendix D) is for programs that provide meals or snacks for their children. All costs for food go on this line. Finally, all consumable items, such as paper towels, paper plates, disposable silverware, foil, and so on go on the "consumables" cost line.

Tips from the Field

✓ Use a different brand, size, or color of paper towels for food service to distinguish them from paper towels used for cleaning supplies.

✓ When you buy multiple items on the same invoice or receipt for various budget line items, highlight these purchases in different colors to indicate which purchase belongs in which category.

LEARNING MATERIAL COSTS

The next cost line item in your budget might be learning materials. You will need to consider this category carefully and broadly in order to budget enough money for a year's supply of these materials. A review of last year's actual expenditures along with the average enrollment will give you a good idea of what to budget in this line item. Consider the following costs:

- consumables
- learning materials
- books

Consumables are items that have a limited life span or that are meant for only one use. For instance, paper, paper towels, and tissues are one-use items, while things like glue, pens, markers, crayons, paint, brushes, tissue paper, cotton balls, and yarn have a life span. The more consumables your program uses, the less you have, so you need to replace them. Once you know what your program spent last year on consumables and compare this figure to last year's and this year's enrollments, you will be able to determine whether you need to increase the amount of money allotted for consumables.

Learning materials also include items placed in dramatic play areas, block areas, game areas, science areas, and so forth. Think of learning materials as any items used to teach children something—from understanding feelings to the science of building blocks to buttoning their shirts or tying their shoes. You can list all board games and materials used to make games, as well as the laminating costs for such handmade games, in this budget line item. You can also include all learning software used by the children. All materials and supplies that support the learning process should go in this category.

You might want to list books in a separate line subitem of learning materials. Books include not just the books used by children but also reference books and lesson planning books for staff, assessment tools, and child development books for families and staff. Another item you might add here is any online resource that requires a membership to access information.

Tips from the Field

✓ Maximize your local public library—they can provide a variety of age-appropriate books for your program.

✓ Buy your learning games in bulk to reduce shipping costs and to take advantage of volume discounts.

✓ Buy consumable materials in bulk quarterly rather than yearly to better forecast the amount you need.

✓ Ask families to donate unused or lightly used games and learning materials.

✓ Ask families to donate items from your program's wish list in lieu of giving holiday gifts to staff.

TRANSPORTATION COSTS

Most programs have some type of transportation costs. Following are some of the costs that you could list under this line item of your budget:

- insurance
- vehicle purchase or rental
- fuel
- maintenance
- training and licensing

Transportation occurs in several forms, such as picking up children at their homes, picking up children from school, and taking children on field trips. For programs that rent bus services for their transportation needs, determining this number is easy. Simply multiply the cost per bus by the amount of field trips per year. The costs involved in purchasing a vehicle are considerably more complex. They include monthly payments, insurance, and maintenance. It stands to reason that the newer the vehicle, the lower its maintenance costs will be. However, there is no way to predict whether your vehicle will be involved in an accident. That's why it's a good idea to add the amount of the insurance deductible to the yearly insurance premiums amount in this line item.

If your program owns its own transportation vehicle, it is important to budget for the cost of fuel and maintenance. It will be up to the organization to decide whether to have a gas card or take fuel costs out of petty cash. The credit card approach allows for documentation of locations, days, times, and amounts of fuel purchased. The petty cash allows anyone to purchase fuel when needed. Each approach has its own benefits. In addition to fuel, a program vehicle will need maintenance, such as routine oil changes and brake repairs. Charges for these services can vary, so do some research to get the best deal. It is important to keep all records of ongoing maintenance. The manufacturer's maintenance recommendations are always a good place to start.

Another consideration is what type of license the driver of the vehicle needs for transporting children for a child- or youth-serving organization. Some states are moving toward a commercial driver's license (CDL) for people transporting children in a fifteen-passenger vehicle. This type of license costs more than a license for driving an ordinary motor vehicle. Determine what type of license your program's driver(s) will need and the cost associated with that as you determine what to allocate for this line subitem. Your organization will need to decide whether to pay the additional CDL cost. Different US states require different types of driver training. Once you know what is required and the cost of such training, list that cost in this category.

Tips from the Field

✓ Collaborate with your local school district to provide busing for field trips.

✓ Make sure whomever you contract for transportation meets all local, state, and federal legal requirements regarding insurance, licensure, medical exams, and so on. Stipulate these requirements in your contract.

✓ Make sure you have signed releases from all families stating that your program is allowed to transport their children. Make sure that the release states the day, time, and destination for each trip.

✓ Avoid using blanket transportation release forms.

✓ When contracting for transportation services, ask for a letter from the service provider's auto insurance company for the beginning and ending dates of coverage. Ask to be notified if there is any change in coverage.

INSURANCE COSTS

Insurance is essential to running any business. You'll need a line item in your budget to track the various types of insurance your program carries. Here are three types of insurance commonly carried by child- and youth-serving organizations:

- liability
- building
- transportation

Liability insurance comes in two forms: general liability and professional liability. General liability insurance protects the insured from liabilities associated with lawsuits. Professional liability insurance helps protect an individual who provides professional services or advice that is deemed negligent by a client or parent and prevents having to bear the full cost of litigation. It is important that child- and youth-serving programs have both types of insurance. All organizations should have a general liability insurance to protect the organization as a whole. Some child- and youth-serving organizations opt for blanket professional liability insurance, which covers all staff during their work time. This type of professional liability insurance is very costly, and the organization needs to be diligent with filing paperwork as employees enter and leave the program. Other programs provide staff with individual policies subsidized by the program. Still others provide liability insurance only for administrative staff. You should list all policy premiums under the liability insurance subitem.

Building insurance is insurance your organization buys to cover damage to the facility due to fire, theft, and so on. The type and scope of building insurance you need depends on whether you own or rent your building. If you own the building, you will need a comprehensive insurance policy that covers not only the building but also its contents, plus a personal injury rider. If you are renting the building, you will need to determine what type of building insurance the owner carries. Often the owner of a building insures only the structure and not the contents or any personal injury resulting from covered damage. If that is the case for your building, you will need to purchase insurance that covers replacement of contents and personal injury costs. Sit down with your program's current insurance agent to determine what your building coverage includes and what the premiums are for that specific coverage. Enter that figure under the building insurance line subitem. Prices for building insurance vary from year to year, so it is wise to have a conversation with your insurance agent to get an estimate for the coming year before allotting money for this cost.

If your program has a vehicle used to transport children to and from specific locations during regular program hours, you need vehicle insurance. There are five main types of vehicle insurance. They are liability, collision, comprehensive, personal injury, and uninsured motorist insurance. Auto liability insurance provides financial protection for the driver who, while operating the vehicle, harms another person or another person's property. Collision auto insurance protects your car if it is damaged by another car or stationary object. Comprehensive auto insurance protects your car from damage other than a collision, such as theft, fire, or a tree falling on top of it. Personal injury auto insurance is available in some states and covers medical expenses, lost wages, and other related costs. Uninsured motorist insurance pays for medical bills resulting from an auto accident cause by a motorist without insurance. It is important to know what insurance your state department of motor vehicles requires for transporting children. Once you have this information, check with your insurance agent to determine the costs for the type of insurance needed. Vehicle insurance premiums can change from year to year, and the costs vary from company to company. Costs are based on the type of insurance purchased and the out-of-pocket deductible chosen. It will be up to you to decide what type of vehicle insurance and deductible your program needs. Some insurance companies offer multiple-policy discounts. It's a good idea to review your vehicle policy coverage and corresponding premiums yearly with your insurance agent. Place the yearly cost for vehicle insurance in this line subitem.

Tips from the Field

✓ Make sure your insurance coverage is adequate, not minimal.

✓ Review your policy limits to make sure they are appropriate for today's market.

✓ If you have a question, ask it.

✓ Remember that insurance coverage can be renegotiated.

✓ Have someone with legal expertise review any insurance contract you sign.

ACCREDITATION COSTS

Accreditation costs vary based on the accrediting organization. (For more information on the many national accrediting bodies, please see chapter 14.) If you are planning to apply to an accrediting organization, place the application fee under this line item. As your program works through the self-study and prepares for the site visit, you should list the additional costs for programming supplies and materials to achieve accreditation here, too. This is also the place to enter costs associated with hiring more staff to meet the staff-child ratio required for accreditation. It typically takes more than a year to complete the accreditation process. The length of the process varies from organization to organization. List accreditation process costs in a separate line item until you achieve accreditation in order to determine the actual cost of accreditation. Once you've achieved accreditation, transfer the additional costs for staff and materials to the staff costs and learning materials line items.

Tips from the Field

✓ Do your research, and know the costs before committing to accreditation.

✓ Shop for accreditation. Several options exist; choose the one that is best for your organization.

✓ Look for accreditation assistance projects that can offer support through the process for little or no cost.

LONG-TERM CAPITAL PROJECTS

Many programs do not include a line item for long-term capital projects in their budgets. However, it is important to plan for the future and to be ready for unexpected events. This line item is typically used for major renovations and other major replacement expenses. While you may not be looking to do a major renovation this year, putting away money over time for a project such as a new playground, new refrigerators, or a new heating system will prevent financial stress when the time comes for that project. By intentionally allocating money— even a small amount—to this line item, you will create a financial safety net for unexpected expenses. Some programs use a saving system to accumulate money for needed repairs, but it is also important to project what you will be putting into this fund. You can use a capital projects line item to do just that. Use this line item from year to year until you have completed the capital project.

Tips from the Field

✓ Be realistic about the replacement costs for major mechanicals.

✓ It's better to have too much money allocated than not enough.

✓ The reality is you cannot fix everything at once. Prioritize.

✓ When you're replacing a major mechanical, shop around for the best deal on the best quality.

✓ Be a good steward of the money allocated; do not spend money just to spend money. If an improvement costs less than you budgeted, reallocate the money to another project.

✓ Putting away a little each month is better than going into debt if something needs to be replaced.

Once your budget is complete, it is wise to share it with your staff. This sends the message that you are transparent. Often employees have no idea how much money is spent in the everyday running of the program, let alone what is spent to support their professional development and classroom activities. One director was faced with cutting costs or shutting the doors. While she labored over the budget, she concluded that she had to find a way to reduce the program's health-care costs to balance the current budget. When she took the budget to her staff and asked for suggestions to reduce costs and increase enrollment in the future to keep the doors open, they understood and took over partial payment of their health-care insurance premiums and outlined a marketing plan to increase enrollment. The program now has a waiting list and provided its staff with a year-end bonus to offset their health-care costs. Your employees can be a valuable source of ideas and support when you trust them and make them a part of the financial stability of your program.

Understanding Revenue

Do not tell me what you value, show me your budget
and I will tell you what you value.

JOE BIDEN, SPEECH AT NATIONAL JEWISH DEMOCRATIC COUNCIL'S WASHINGTON POLICY CONFERENCE

Now that you have a handle on how to create a proposed budget and project expenditures, you will need to take time to understand the revenue streams that generate money for operating your program. The biggest revenue stream is likely the fees paid for services you provide (called fee for service, program fees, or tuition). However, this is probably not your only revenue stream. Child- and youth-serving organizations often do not take in enough money from program fees to cover the actual cost of running their programs. A little creative thinking and tapping into outside resources can create a variety of revenue streams, including the following:

- grants
- in-kind donations
- Quality Rating and Improvement System
- federal child care subsidy
- Child and Adult Care Food Program
- fee for service

To develop a fee structure, you will first need to know three things: your projected expenditures, how much money (revenue) will be coming into your program, and your projected enrollment. Since you have spent time creating a proposed budget, you already have a good idea of your overall expenditures. Let's continue by examining your potential revenue streams, then your projected enrollment.

GRANTS

Grants—small and large—can form an additional revenue stream. For example, if you receive a grant for a special learning project, you will not have to fund that project out of pocket, and this will reduce your learning materials cost. If you receive money for a new playground, the money you had allocated for it can now be reallocated to other things. But many program directors shy away from grants, either because they are not grant writers or because they do not know where to start. You needn't let either of these obstacles get in your way.

Most libraries offer grant-writing seminars at little or no cost. In addition, many libraries have a person on staff who specializes in grant writing. Often this person is called the grant librarian. First, determine what you would like a grant to fund. For instance, if you want to teach children about gardening or bring in special gardening programs, you might look for a small local grant that has funded such projects in the past. For a larger grant, such as one to build a new playground or make your program more accessible for children with disabilities, the grant librarian can help you identify potential grant opportunities. A grant librarian can also help you access its Foundation Center subscription and help you get started at www.foundationcenter.org. This website offers free training, articles, podcasts, and more to help you build your fundraising, grant-writing, leadership, and management skills. With a subscription, you can also use this site to search foundations by type, city, funding areas, and past grantees. You can also look to the wider Internet to determine who funds what in your community. Local foundations, Lions Clubs, Kiwanis Clubs, and Rotary Clubs are great places to start. In addition, the Grant Professionals Association (www.grantprofessionals .org) has chapters all over the country, and its meetings are usually open to non-members. Attending a meeting can give you an opportunity to meet and learn from experienced grant writers. You might also find a grant professional who works independently for a fee or someone who's willing to help you write a small grant or two pro bono. For some directors, it's helpful to hire a part-time grant writer to help write their first grant.

Grant applications vary in length and requirements. Read the directions, and follow them. Give funders what they ask for. If a funder wants you to discuss your project in five pages, then do it in five pages. If this is your first time writing a grant, stick to smaller community foundations that may want only a letter outlining your request. Most grants—large or small—ask for a short narrative that explains the project's purpose, expected learning goals, and benefit to the community. Larger grants may ask for program history and description as well as your organization's vision and mission statements. It is important to have a project budget that lists all the costs associated with the project, from what will be purchased to transportation. For instance, if the grant is to take children on a field trip, the cost should include your time for staff supervision, staff preparation for the trip, transportation costs, entrance fees, and food and drink. You may also be able to include costs for advertising the trip and printing permission slips. Find out for sure whether you're allowed to use grant money for staff time and organizational overhead before including these costs in the project budget for your grant application. Applications for larger grants can be overwhelming if you have never written a grant before, so take your time. The more dollars you ask for, the more detailed information may be required. It is standard, regardless of the size of the grant, for the funder to ask for some type of report describing how the grant money was spent and its overall benefit to the program and community.

Tips from the Field

✓ Before you start looking for grant opportunities, decide how much time and money you want to spend on that research. You could use free search databases, or you could invest some money in fee- or subscription-based search databases.

✓ If grant writing is new to you, start with a small community foundation. Smaller foundations often have easier application requirements.

✓ Don't waste your time trying to find funds for general operating support. Foundations that support this are rare.

✓ Remember that even grant money is not completely free. Most grants will want the grantee to have some money in the game, such as finding other partners to help fund the project or using staff time to administer the grant.

✓ After you hear a funder's decision, write a note to the funder thanking its officers for the opportunity to submit—even if your proposal has been denied. Remember, the foundation officers and board members took time to read your proposal. Your note will set you apart. Few people write thank-you notes for accepted proposals; even fewer write notes when they are denied.

✓ Even if you do not get funded, add the foundation to your newsletter mailing list.

If you do not receive the first grant you apply for, do not be discouraged. Many seasoned grant writers have had their requests denied. You can usually contact a foundation officer and ask why you were not funded. Do this in the spirit of wanting to hone your grant-writing skills. Be aware that some foundations will not answer this question. If that is the case, do not push them; simply thank them for their time. There are many reasons why great proposals don't get funded. It may be that another issue within the community is more pressing. Or perhaps there were three times more proposals than available money. The reasons can be endless. If you do call a foundation looking for reasons, be calm and respectful. The last thing you want to do is offend or anger a foundation officer. These professionals network with one another, and you do not want to be a negative topic at the next local meeting.

Above all, remember that relationships are important. Do not send your application without a call first. Make a quick call to the program officer to discuss what you are planning to propose and why you feel it is needed. It is better for the officer to have had advance contact with you than to receive a blind proposal from you. Keep in touch with the officer throughout the year. Don't communicate only when you want money. Introduce yourself when you attend similar meetings. Everyone wants to match a name with a face. If a foundation funds your request, provide regular updates on your project. Send pictures and notes from children and families. Also be aware that some foundations do not want you to contact them before submission or after awards have been granted. Check applications, foundation information, and websites to see if they specifically request no contact. If they do state that, *do not contact them*.

IN-KIND DONATIONS

Another great way to help balance your budget is through in-kind donations. For example, large companies replace computers regularly. If your program is on the recipient list for a company's computer donation program, you could reduce the cost of purchasing new computers for your facility, freeing up money for other areas.

You can begin your search for in-kind donations by asking your children's family members where they work. Find out whether their companies can donate anything helpful to your program. For instance, if a parent works at a big-box hardware store, the store might be able to donate scrap wood for the woodworking area. If another relative works for a paper company, the company may be able to donate paper for your art and writing centers. Perhaps someone works in an office, and that company could donate old file folders to make folder games or to create child and staff files.

Do not always rely on families to make these contacts. Look outside your families to companies in the larger community for potential donations. You can make a call or visit a company that has something you need. For instance, let's say your preschool room would like carpet squares for the children to use during group time. Call a local carpet distributer and ask what happens to old carpet samples when a new line of carpets come in. Explain who you are and what you would be using the carpet samples for. Offer to give the company a tax write-off letter for the donation.

Some companies engage in community service projects, such as repainting rooms, spreading mulch on playgrounds, or building playgrounds. To tap into this resource, create a flyer outlining donations your program is looking for, along with a cover letter that describes your program, and send it to local companies. This type of communication offers two benefits. First, it gives you the opportunity to talk about your program and the services you offer, thus marketing your program. Second, you give companies a local organization with which they can conduct some community service or to which they can donate unused materials and supplies.

In-kind donations like the ones described in this section reduce spending in various budget categories, freeing up money to be spent in other areas. Finding these in-kind opportunities takes time, but the effort is worthwhile. Participating in community events and meetings related to child and family services can help you develop relationships. These relationships, in turn, may in the future support your program by informing you of training opportunities or telling you about upcoming grants. An in-kind donation can be a win-win for both your organization and the contributing company.

Becoming visible in the local community can be a slow process. Even when you invite community leaders into your program, they may not come—but do not give up. Use some of the following tips to help you get people in the door. And when they do come or offer services, send thank-you notes from the children. It is these handmade notes that donors cherish most. Include pictures of the children using provided supplies or participating in the activities or event that companies or community leaders supported. This approach goes a long way in cementing relationships and opening the door for additional donations. In short, make your program visible to community leaders, and make them want to be associated with your program.

Tips from the Field

✓ Check with your local United Way office and your community's chamber of commerce to determine whether any local companies are looking for community service opportunities.

✓ Speak at Kiwanis Club, Lions Club, or Rotary Club meetings about your program.

✓ Invite local community and business leaders into your program so they remember it when dollars become available.

✓ Send local leaders your monthly newsletter.

✓ Create an event, and invite local leaders to come.

✓ Place articles in the local newspaper about the great things you are doing in your program.

QUALITY RATING AND IMPROVEMENT SYSTEM

Many states have a Quality Rating and Improvement System (QRIS) for child- and youth-serving programs. A QRIS is usually a voluntary program designed to recognize child care centers, family child care programs, and after-school programs that exceed the quality benchmarks outlined in licensing regulations. These standards can vary widely from state to state. Find out if your state has a QRIS by searching on the Internet. The search words *quality rating and improvement system* and the name of your state should show you whether this system exists in your state. Once you have identified the system for your state, determine what types of child- and youth-serving programs it includes. Not all states that have a QRIS offer it for after-school programs or family child care. Learn the requirements within your state, and find out how to apply for the process. A QRIS is usually linked to a state licensing agency.

Each system has several levels of achievement that exceed state requirements. The top level usually meets or exceeds nationally recognized accreditation standards. Most states have a document that lists what is required to achieve each level within the system. Review this document to determine what you have already accomplished and what you need to do to achieve your desired level. Most state QRISs conduct a desk review. This review examines the administrative side of your program, including policies and procedures. In addition, a site visit is usually conducted to determine whether the day-to-day programming meets the indicators listed in each level. In some states, coaching, additional funding, training, technical assistance, and resources are provided for each level achieved at no cost to the program. In addition, some states are tying child care subsidy reimbursement rates to QRIS levels. Dollars received for training and coaching opportunities are dollars that do not have to be allocated in your budget for professional development, freeing them up for things like staff raises, program materials, and supplies.

Tips from the Field

✓ When you begin the QRIS process, take it slow. Attend informational classes, and ask questions.

✓ Learn how the QRIS in your state supports the ongoing development of your program.

✓ Use the documents for QRIS desk review to create a manual outlining processes, times, and documents used for your program's operational tasks.

✓ If your state QRIS program provides an annual stipend, use it to give yearly bonuses for staff.

✓ Seek out other administrators who have gone through the QRIS process, and attend local networking meetings to find support.

FEDERAL CHILD CARE SUBSIDY

The Child Care and Development Fund (CCDF) child care subsidy is a program sponsored by the US Department of Health and Human Services and administered by the Office of Child Care (OCC). OCC (2016) "supports low-income working families through child care financial assistance and promotes children's learning by improving the quality of early care and education and afterschool programs." The purpose of this program is to provide children with high-quality, affordable child- and youth-serving programs. The subsidy offsets the cost of child care for the family while paying the program a predetermined cost of care allocation per qualifying child. To determine the cost of care, some states conduct a market survey among care providers. Using the data received from child and youth providers, the state will set a fee per qualifying child. Each state or territory establishes its own eligibility policies and cost for care reimbursed to programs, and has a designated grantee that administers the subsidy funds.

It's a good idea to know your state or territory's CCDF subsidy amount when you create your budget. If your program accepts the federal child care subsidy, subsidy fees can provide consistent funding and limit families defaulting on payments. Contact your state or territory's grantee to determine current eligibility, reimbursement rate, how to apply, policies, and procedures. For a complete list of CCDF grantees, visit www.acf.hhs.gov/programs/occ/resource /ccdf-grantee-state-and-territory-contacts. Many states offer local training for new programs. Some allow you to sign up for ongoing updates as things change and clarifications are needed. When problems arise or you are in doubt, ask questions. Do not wait. Waiting can cause you to miss a deadline and lose funding for a child or children. While all states require constant staff oversight and paperwork submission, you can do a lot of this work online. This makes it easy to adjust your paperwork as children enter and leave your program.

Tips from the Field

✓ Enroll in a training that explains what is expected of your program when you provide federally subsidized child care services, such as what you can and cannot do, the family enrollment process, and how and when to file reports.

✓ Keep receipts of payment for each family payment, regardless of the amount.

✓ Use only debit cards and money orders for any type of payment, because these methods provide a built-in payment tracking system.

✓ Balance subsidized families with fee-paying families to maintain a constant revenue stream and sustain longevity.

✓ Assign one person to oversee the daily attendance of children on subsidy, so you can make necessary corrections quickly and avoid missing any income.

CHILD AND ADULT CARE FOOD PROGRAM

The Child and Adult Care Food Program (CACFP) is a revenue stream that provides nutritious foods and positive outcomes for children. Through CACFP, 3.3 million children receive nutritious snacks and meals each day (USDA 2015). CACFP is a federal program funded through the US Department of Agriculture (USDA) Office of Food and Nutrition Service. The program designates an agency within each state or territory to administer the food program within its borders. State and territory agencies then typically subcontract with local agencies that monitor compliance and conduct site visits. This program reimburses child- and youth-serving programs for the cost of food prepared for and consumed by the children within their care who meet particular criteria.

CACFP is designed to serve the neediest children. It is meant to improve the food served to children. Families must complete an income eligibility application and an enrollment form annually. Reimbursement is based on a tiered system. The amount of reimbursement varies based on the tier in which the program qualifies. In-home providers can qualify if they live near a school that serves fifty or more children free lunch or qualify based on their income or census information. Centers need to meet the definition of a child care center and must have a certain percentage of children who qualify for free and reduced-price meals or receive benefit from Title XX of the Social Security Act as defined in the CACFP regulations. After-school programs may qualify for some meal and snack reimbursement for children up to twelve years old based on the children's eligibility. (Families must fill out enrollment forms to ascertain that information.) New reimbursement rates are posted each year at www.fns.usda.gov/cacfp/reimbursement-rates. The rates are effective from July 1 of one year to June 30 of the following year.

You can locate a sponsoring agency that serves your location by visiting www.fns.usda.gov/cacfp/cacfp-contacts. The resources offered vary from agency to agency. However, the Team Nutrition section of the USDA website (www.fns.usda.gov/tn) provides many resources for centers, schools, and family child care providers. The type and scope of training also vary from agency to agency. Some agencies offer face-to-face training, others offer webinars, and still others offer online classes. Check with your local sponsoring agency to determine what coaching, training, and resource materials it offers.

To create menus, you can use meal pattern charts provided by your sponsoring agency or find charts at www.fns.usda.gov/cacfp/meals-and-snacks. To make meal planning, substitutions, and documentation easier, you can use a meal-planning software such as Minute Menu. You must keep receipts for food purchased and turn them in monthly. If your program is purchasing a variety of items, place all CACFP items first at the checkout and have the cashier subtotal these items before ringing up other program materials. This will make tallying and turning in receipts easier.

Some of the biggest compliance issues include documenting point of service, being out of ratio, forgetting to document substitutions on the menu, and communicating when your schedule has changed or when you will not have children in care. Point-of-service documentation is the process of recording what you are serving at the time you are serving it. This documentation is required of programs that care for twelve or more children. Those serving fewer children (usually family child care providers) have until the end of their business day to record their meals.

Staff from your sponsoring CACFP agency will conduct several compliance visits per year to your program. When conducting a visit, the agency staff needs to observe mealtime with children in attendance, so it is important to let them know when your program will be without children. These staff are mandated reporters. That means they are required to report to a program's licensing agency when a program is out of adult-child ratio or when children are in danger. If your program has been declared seriously deficient, it will be placed on the national disqualifying list and will be unable to receive federal CACFP dollars for seven years.

Tips from the Field

✓ Look to your local CACFP agencies for resources.

✓ Create a preapproved eight-week rotating menu so that you are using creditable food and are always in compliance.

✓ Enter your enrollment daily at the point of service.

✓ Be on-site during mealtimes, or communicate with your sponsoring agency when you will be out of the program.

✓ Find out whether your sponsoring agency is using specific software to input menus and document enrollment. If so, use the same software.

✓ Include declaration of income forms in your program enrollment packets.

FEE FOR SERVICE

To determine your fee for service (tuition or program fees), you will need to project your enrollment. A good rule of thumb is to project enrollment at 85 percent of your maximum licensed capacity, even if you have been full for the past few years. Enrollment fluctuates, so using your maximum licensed capacity to project income could put you in the red. If you remain full the entire year, and fee-for-service revenue is more than projected, you can reallocate those funds to long-term projects, staff incentives, or other areas that need additional funds.

Chapter 8 and the earlier sections of chapter 9 discuss all the information you need to determine what your fee for service should be so your program can remain in the black. Once you have plugged into your budget all your projected expenditures, you can subtract your revenue streams for the budget year to find out how much revenue you still need. Divide this needed revenue by 85 percent of your maximum enrollment. Next, divide that number by fifty weeks. (That's right—fifty, not fifty-two.) Using fifty weeks rather than fifty-two provides a built-in cost-of-living increase. See the following example:

$650,000.00	**Total projected expenditures**
– $10,000.00 (grant)	Subtract revenue streams.
– $75,000.00 (CCDF subsidy)	
– $30,000.00 (CACFP)	
= $535,000.00	**Revenue needed**
÷ 102	Divide revenue needed by number of children at 85% of maximum enrollment.
= $5,245.00	**Revenue needed per child**
÷ 50	Divide revenue needed per child by 50 weeks.
= $105.00	**Per-child, full-time (5 days per week) fee for service**

This program's fee for service equals $105 per child for a full-time (five days per week) slot. If the program offers part-time options, it can divide that weekly fee by five to determine a daily fee. Using this method, a child attending this program would pay $21 for one day, $42 for two days, and so on. Some centers use a different approach to calculate part-time fees. They encourage families to enroll in more days by having a higher daily rate for part-time enrollment than for full-time enrollment, making the latter a better value. If the program provides a multiple-children discount, this discount must figure into the fee for service as well.

Tips from the Field

✔ Take time to run the numbers.

✔ Figuring the actual cost of care takes time, but it is one of the most important steps toward fiscal security.

✔ Communicate to families why fees may need to be raised. Show them the expenditures and the current fee schedule, and communicate the shortfall.

✔ Educate your staff about the budget, and make them aware of any needed change in program fees.

PART 3

Finding the Right Staff

Finding the right staff is the key to success for a child- or youth-serving program. By investing time and effort in advertising, screening, and selecting staff, you can build a cohesive and effective workforce. Putting together a team that is professional, educated, and caring creates a program where families want to place their children and where children want to be. Each step in the process needs to be purposeful and should provide information you need to make a hiring decision. Advance planning and communicating clear job expectations can bring you just the right candidate for your program.

10

Hiring

No matter how good or successful you are or how clever or crafty, your business and its future are in the hands of the people you hire.

AKIO MORITA, *MADE IN JAPAN*

To find the right staff, you need to know what you are looking for in an employee. You may feel tempted to shortchange this process if you are understaffed and need to fill a spot to meet a local, state, or organizational requirement. But remember that of all the processes discussed in this book, this one is by far the most important to maintaining a successful organization. Reflect on your organizational mission, and create a list of characteristics needed to achieve that mission. Once you have your list of characteristics, you can decide what skills you already have with existing staff and what skills are still missing. For example, if your accreditation requires that all your staff be degreed, then look at the types of degrees and skill sets associated with those degrees and advertise for those skill sets. If you are looking for someone whose primary job will be to seek funding to support your organization, then advertise for someone who has grant-writing or fundraising experience.

YOUR STAFFING NEEDS

Advance planning is the key. If you are proactive prior to a vacancy, you will be ready to advertise immediately for what you need and want rather than scrambling to find a warm body to fill the spot. Begin by creating a file that contains a folder for each type of staff you currently employ and types whom you may need in the future, such as clerical assistant, classroom lead, education coordinator, community outreach person, human resources manager, grant writer, and so on. Now look at the job descriptions you reviewed or created in chapter 1 for each type of job in your program. The skill sets needed should be apparent when you read these job descriptions. Ask yourself the following questions:

- What skills are needed to accomplish the tasks listed on the job description?

- What education is required?

- What type of personality do new staff need in order to get along with the existing staff?

- What types of experience and length of experience are acceptable for your organization?

Because you are planning for future hires, there's no need to rush. Work on this task in stages. Once you have done the initial work, let it sit, and review it in a few days. When you are satisfied with your work, create a brief ad for each position. Remember to mention in your advertisement nonnegotiables such as minimum education required, work hours, or valid driver's license.

To minimize downtime in looking for a new employee, create a list of where you will advertise along with the contact information for those places. Look to local colleges, as most college students want some job experience before they graduate. Colleges that offer health and human services, education, or early childhood degrees are great places to start. Community newspapers are affordable venues to place ads. Churches and community organizations that have newsletters or bulletins can also lead you to high-quality staff. Some child- and youth-serving programs look to online advertising of job openings. Another option is to reach out to your program's board members and current staff and ask them to publicize your open position. If you choose this option, provide the current job description that outlines the job duties, so there will not be a misunderstanding about what is expected from a candidate in the open position. It is always a good idea to develop relationships with those with whom you plan on posting a job opening. It is easier to ask a favor from someone who knows you than from someone who doesn't.

Tips from the Field

✔ Plan for an opening before the opening occurs.

✔ Advertise for what you need.

✔ Have someone else read your advertisement to make sure your words say what you intended.

✔ Place ads for job openings with community organizations.

✔ Look for college students who need to complete a practicum or community service hours.

THE JOB APPLICATION

It is just as important to customize the job application as it is to customize the job posting. Reviewing the existing job application will help you answer the following questions:

- Does the job application look professional, with your organization's logo and address?

- What questions do you ask? Are they appropriate for the position you have open?

- Have you taken time to decide what the appropriate answers for these questions are?

- What questions need to be added?

As you think about the last bullet point, you might want to add questions such as the following:

- Have you ever been convicted of a crime (misdemeanor or felony)? If so, explain.

- Do you have reliable transportation to and from our location?

- Have you ever applied to this organization before? If so, when?

- Do you have family or friends who have worked or are currently working for our organization? If so, list their names below.

- Are you willing to submit to a random drug test?

- What skills do you bring from your last position that would be helpful in the position for which you are now applying?

- Do you need reasonable accommodations to complete the job responsibilities? If so, please explain.

- Are you able to work overtime if needed?

If after reviewing the application you feel it needs an overhaul, you can find online many job application templates that you can customize and print for general use. Looking at these templates might also provide you with additional questions for your job application if you are planning to revise an existing one. When you are creating questions for a job application or interview, be aware of what you can and cannot ask an applicant. You cannot ask applicants their race, sexual orientation, religion, nation of origin, disability status, or if they are pregnant or intend to become pregnant, to name just a few. For more information on prohibited questions and practices, visit the US Equal Employment Opportunity Commission (EEOC) website at www.eeoc.gov/laws/practices/. Some other things you may want to put on your application are your organization's mission and vision statements, your program's long-range goals, contact information, an equal opportunity employer statement, and an employment-at-will statement. Please see appendix F for a sample generic staff job application.

Once you've finished creating an application, the next step is to establish an application process. How will your applicants receive the application, and how will they return it to you? E-mail, snail mail, and online submission are all possibilities. Online submission allows you to get applications quickly; however, it does take time to create the profile and upload the application.

Tips from the Field

✔ Place ads in newspapers, on social media such as Twitter and Facebook, and on your community's college job board.

✔ Tell community leaders you are hiring.

✔ Ask only questions to which you want answers; do not ask questions that have no relevance to the job duties.

THE INTERVIEW

There are three main types of interviews: phone interviews, face-to-face interviews, and skills application interviews. Each type provides the interviewer with specific information about the candidate. Before you schedule interviews, of course, it is important to review the written applications you've received.

When you receive an application, read it carefully. First, ask yourself if anything on the application would disqualify the applicant. For instance, if your program's license requires a high school diploma or equivalent to work in the advertised job, and an applicant does not have that, then do not interview that applicant. Next, rank the application among all the applications you've received. When ranking an application, consider whether the applicant meets all the criteria needed to work in your organization, follows instructions, provides requested information, and writes clearly and understandably. This strategy will provide insight as to the applicant's attention to detail and willingness to take direction. Make note of additional information you need and clarification questions you'd like to ask.

Once you have ranked all the applications, choose which applicants you would like to interview by phone. The purpose of phone interviews is to do an initial screening, to confirm basic information and criteria needed for the job, and to ask clarification questions about statements on the application. Phone interviews can help you narrow the field of candidates and get more information about them, such as their past experiences with children and families from diverse backgrounds or whether they are self-starters. In addition, phone interviews can help you can gauge how candidates' personal skills and knowledge mesh with your organizational philosophy. Write down your phone interview questions, and ask all candidates the same questions. Questions should be open-ended; that is, they should require the candidate to talk and require you to listen. If you want more information on a particular subject, say, "Tell me more about that," or "How do you feel that experience will help you in this position?" (For several sample phone interview questions, please see appendix G.)

When the phone interviews are over, you will be able to choose candidates who should come in for face-to-face interviews. Face-to-face interviews can be either group interviews or one-on-one interviews. Each type of interview serves a specific purpose.

There are two types of group interviews. One type takes place with several other applicants. All the candidates chosen for face-to-face interviews gather in a room at your facility, in a restaurant, at a coffee shop, or the like with you and a staff person. Each candidate is asked a question, and after the candidate answers, the other candidates can comment. This approach helps you see how succinctly candidates can answer under pressure. It also helps you observe how candidates get along with others, identify their communication skills, and assess their interests, professional style, problem-solving skills, and overall attitude. The second type of group interview is called a staff interview. Several of a candidate's potential coworkers meet with the candidate and ask a set of predetermined questions. These questions can reveal how a candidate views children and can demonstrate the candidate's competency. This approach also helps you determine whether the applicant is a good fit for that work group.

The most popular type of interview is the one-on-one interview between you and a candidate. Make sure you come to the table prepared. Have a list of questions you feel are important for a candidate to answer. These questions should help you evaluate a candidate's competencies and expectations. (For a list of sample one-on-one interview questions, please see appendix H.) Think ahead of time about what you consider appropriate answers to those questions. Sorting this out in advance will help you choose the candidate who best fits the culture and purpose of your program.

Face-to-face interviews will help you choose candidates who should come in for skills application interviews, or "working interviews." This kind of interview takes time, but it allows you to see candidates in action. It can help you not only assess their skills but also observe how comfortable they are in your setting and how they interact with children, staff, and families. You might have a candidate present an age-appropriate lesson plan or conduct an activity. Some states require candidates to complete specific training before participating in a skills application interview, even if they are not left alone with the children. If this is the case in your state, you should tell candidates about it during the screening process. After a candidate undergoes a working interview in the classroom, have staff, administrators, and families answer a few questions about their observations. (Please see appendix I for sample questions.)

Tips from the Field

✓ Look beyond candidates' documentation, and ask yourself: Was their appearance appropriate for the position? Were they on time? Did they follow directions? Did they come prepared for the interview?

✓ Remember that new staff need to mesh with your program's existing staff, culture, families, and community.

✓ Not choosing the right person can undo your program's culture and the cohesiveness of your team.

INTERVIEWING DOS AND DON'TS

How you ask questions and what you do and don't ask are important aspects of any interview. If you write down your questions prior to an interview, you reduce your chances of asking inappropriate questions. During the interview, stick to what you wrote. At the end, ask, "Is there anything else you would like us to know about you?" The answers you receive to this question can be informative, because it allows candidates to share information about themselves that they deem important.

There are many questions you may not ask a candidate in an interview. For instance, you may ask a candidate, "Is there another name that you would like to be called or that people call you?" If you ask this question, then you can be sure to use the correct name when you check the candidate's references. You *may not*, however, ask candidates about their nationality, religion, or race (just to name a few). If you have any doubts about questions you can or can't ask, visit the US Equal Employment Opportunity Commission at www.eeoc.gov/laws/practices/. This website has a searchable data system so you can find information easily and quickly.

Tips from the Field

✓ Stick to the questions you have prepared.

✓ Make sure you know what you can and cannot ask.

✓ Ask all candidates the same questions.

CHECKING REFERENCES

As you narrow your pool of candidates, you should ask for references—and you should check them. References help you verify the information provided by candidates and make sure they are qualified for the position. References also help you learn more about candidates and see if they are a good fit. Professional references or letters of recommendation are preferable to personal references. A reference from a previous employer or professional colleague can give insight into a candidate's work ethic. One question can tell you volumes: Would you hire this individual again?

Past employers can answer questions as long as their answers are factual and bear no malice toward their former employee. However, some employers will not answer questions about former employees because they fear defamation lawsuits. Many organizations will not give references of any kind. Others will refer you to a staff member who may provide little or no information in order to avoid legal issues. Consider having candidates sign a waiver that allows your organization to contact past employers and that indicates candidates will not hold your organization accountable for information provided by past employers. If a company will give a reference, be sure to verify education, past job experience, longevity of employment, job title, salary, and duties performed. Remember that you cannot ask about race, age, gender, disability, nationality, religion, political affiliation, or sexual orientation.

In addition to checking references, consider conducting criminal background checks, drug testing, verification of US citizenship, and credit checks (for those who might have access to program money). Background checks are especially important, even if your licensing or accreditation does not require them. Some programs conduct only a local background check, but a state background check is a much safer choice. If your program is close to a state line, you should also conduct a background check in the bordering state. It is really easy to drive a few miles across a state line to get a job. A multistate background check is more expensive, but it is money well spent to protect the safety of your program's children and staff. At minimum, you should conduct a background check for the candidate's state of residence and the state in which your program is located.

Tips from the Field

✓ When you're checking references, ask about the candidate's skills.

✓ Ask candidates for a copy of their driver's license or state identification card.

✓ Make sure candidates know that if you hire them, you will require proof of citizenship.

✓ Have candidates sign a waiver giving you permission to check social media and talk to previous employers.

EFFECTIVE ORIENTATION

The first opportunity to make sure a new employee understands your job expectations is during staff orientation. Staff orientation isn't cheap; it takes materials and staff time to plan and conduct orientation, then supervise and mentor the new employee. It takes away time from regularly scheduled work. However, orientation is less expensive than the hiring process. Well-planned and comprehensive orientation, along with providing a new hire with an on-site mentor, has been shown to reduce staff turnover. Because staff turnover creates a huge expense—so big that the repeated costs for hiring and orienting new staff can destroy an organization—comprehensive and proactive reduction of staff turnover is worth the time and money it takes.

When you hire a new employee, it is important to clear your schedule and give that person your focused attention. To avoid overwhelming a new employee, some programs split orientation into several sections over a week. When you deliver information in smaller pieces, the employee has a chance to digest what is being taught and ask clarification questions. Some programs conduct orientation in the morning, and then new staff work in the classroom in the afternoon. This approach allows a new employee to integrate slowly into the program. Other programs have a veteran employee orient the new employee. And some programs provide the new hire with an on-site senior staff mentor who can answer questions as the employee gets familiar with the program's day-to-day workings. Often, talking to a peer mentor is less stressful than talking with an administrator. Some directors review the staff handbook with the new employee page by page, answering questions along the way, in lieu of a formal orientation. Whichever approach you choose, it is important that your new hire receives the first orientation from you, as well as a scheduled follow-up meeting with you one month after hiring, so you can make sure the employee gets accurate information from the very start. The follow-up meeting allows a new employee to check in and clear up any lingering questions.

Use an orientation checklist during the process so you do not get diverted and miss important information. To create this checklist, review your staff handbook and your program's policies and procedures. (For a sample staff orientation checklist, see appendix J.) Sharon Bergen's *Early Childhood Staff Orientation Guide* is another helpful resource that provides strategies for creating and conducting staff orientation. To prepare for the first orientation meeting, create a folder or binder, and in it place information on the items you'll discuss in the order you will address them. Much of what you will discuss is in the staff handbook, but if you note where these items are located in the handbook ahead of time, you can minimize the time spent trying to find it during orientation. At the conclusion of the orientation, you and the new employee should sign and date the orientation checklist to indicate that the employee received an orientation. Give the employee a copy of this document, and place another copy in the staff file.

Tips from the Field

✓ Giving a new employee a thorough orientation can mitigate problems down the road.

✓ Do not shortchange your preparation for an employee's orientation; it will serve as the road map for the new employee.

✓ Provide the handbook and job description in hard copy as well as an electronic version.

Empowering Staff

Surround yourself with the best people you can find, delegate authority, and don't interfere as long as the overall policy that you've decided upon is being carried out.

RONALD REAGAN, "REAGAN ON DECISION-MAKING, PLANNING, GORBACHEV, AND MORE"

As a director, sometimes you may find that your program staff seem lackluster. They do not show any initiative or get-up-and-go. Employees have needs, and when those needs aren't met, they may not feel valued. When individuals do not feel valued, they may think, "Why bother?" When this happens, you must work to empower your staff.

DEVELOPING OWNERSHIP

Developing ownership is key to empowering staff. Employees who realize they are an important part of the program feel a sense of worth that inspires them to do their best. Assess your staff's level of ownership by asking yourself the following questions:

- How do you include staff in program decision making?

- When and how can staff bring concerns to management?

- How do you communicate with staff?

- Do your employees know why things are done the way they are done?

- What are your employees' preferred methods of communication?

- What skills does each employee have?
- Have you tapped into those skills?

Including staff in developing new procedures and solving problems helps them feel respected and develop ownership of the program. Providing staff with a place to give feedback or make suggestions sends a message that you appreciate their comments and prefer not to wait for the next staff meeting to hear and address them. Providing staff with effective ongoing communication about the program allows all staff to be on the same page and helps them feel valued. Providing this information in employees' preferred communication style shows that you respect them as individuals.

It is important for you as an administrator to invest time and resources in your staff. Understand where your employees want to go professionally, and help them get there. When you know what their skills are—and are not—you can create opportunities for employees to shine and to lead. Remember, delegating tasks to staff says you feel they can complete the tasks effectively and on time. Understanding the specific skill set of each employee allows you to tailor opportunities for success. Assigning tasks that employees have the skills to complete successfully creates a sense of self-worth and a belief that they can make a difference. This belief in their abilities increases their sense of ownership and empowerment.

Empowering staff means cooperating with employees even when you feel they are being difficult. Difficult people exist in every job, and child- and youth-serving programs are no exception. You may find that you spend 80 percent of your time dealing with 20 percent of the people in your program. You may wish these people would just go away, but the reality is that even if they did, another 20 percent would take their place. When you're dealing with difficult people, you may feel tempted to respond in kind. Be aware that this type of response can have long-lasting negative repercussions, especially if you are new in your position. People will make note of how you respond to stressful situations and difficult individuals.

To increase your chance of positive results, try to keep a positive attitude. First, be aware of your body language. Your body language says more about how you really feel than your words ever will. Next, take a breath so you have time to formulate an appropriate response to the situation. Begin your response by making sure you know what the problem really is. Restate what you have heard or otherwise observed. Even if you have had a good relationship with the individual prior to the situation at hand, you may still be caught off guard and be too upset or angry to discuss the situation, so give yourself time to process it. For example, if an employee comes to you upset about something a coworker said or did, and you are just finding out about it, you may feel blindsided. Tell the person you will need to investigate this concern and will respond after you've done so. Write down what the upset employee said occurred and what his or her concerns are so that when you investigate, you will not be struggling to recall information. Writing things down will also send a message that you are taking the concerns seriously. Ask clarifying questions if you doubt your understanding of events. As you listen, try to imagine how the concerned person feels, and convey your understanding. Make sure to say when the person will be hearing from you. Always leave the conversation with a statement that says you will work together to figure this out and you are glad the person came to you.

Tips from the Field

✔ To get respect, give it.

✔ Remember that ethics and trust are key to the success of any organization or relationship.

✔ To empower others, share your power.

✔ Do not become power hungry; this hunger will consume you in the end.

✔ Mentor your staff.

✔ Be willing to work together to find solutions to problems.

ESTABLISHING ACCOUNTABILITY

To empower staff, you must not only help them develop ownership but also establish accountability for their choices and actions. Occasionally you'll discover that your staff's choices are not in line with your program's mission or philosophy. Or you may find that your staff thinks you are their parent and should follow them around giving reminders and asking for needed information. To establish accountability, you need to set clear expectations, timelines, and consequences. Set clear expectations right from the start during staff orientation. First, check and see if job descriptions, orientation materials, and program handbooks state clear expectations for specific tasks and consequences for failing those expectations. If not, then these documents need revision to address those issues.

Let's say that your staff handbook clearly states that time sheets for hourly staff are due to you at 9:00 a.m. Monday. This allows you to calculate payroll and send it to the payroll company by 12:00 p.m. so checks can be cut and delivered to your program for Friday distribution. You also remind employees about this deadline at staff meetings. It is not your job to wander around asking for time sheets. If employees fail to turn in their time sheets, the logical consequence is that they do not get their checks on Friday. As long as employees are not out ill on Monday, those are the rules—and the staff must be accountable to the rules. If they forget once, they will surely remember every time thereafter. This example may seem harsh, but the occasional unpleasant consequence can serve as a useful and necessary learning opportunity. If you spend time tracking down each piece of paper you need, you will not have enough time to do your job. On the other hand, this is not something that you want to happen to any of your staff. Perhaps a good topic for a staff meeting might be how to make the time sheet process easier to use or easier to remember. People generally do not argue with rules they set for themselves, so engage your staff in setting procedures and consequences for not following those procedures. This approach sets the stage for self-management.

Tips from the Field

✓ You might think that working with adults will be easier than working with children, because adults know how to act, but realize that adults do have deficiencies.

✓ Repeat the expectation that employees must complete assigned jobs in a timely manner. Adults have busy lives and need to hear expectations more than once.

✓ Use role play or describe scenarios that depict accountability during a staff meeting to encourage discussion and problem solving.

✓ Including staff in establishing policy and procedures can increase compliance.

Handbooks

A memorandum is written not to inform the reader but to protect the writer.

DEAN ACHESON, *WALL STREET JOURNAL*

Handbooks set expectations for both families and staff. To some directors, developing handbooks may seem like a questionable use of time. However, the time and effort you invest to provide up-to-date policies and procedures will protect your organization, your staff, and your program's children. Most state regulatory agencies and all accrediting bodies require handbooks in some form. While national accrediting bodies have specific guidelines regarding what should be addressed in handbooks, some states have fewer requirements.

Handbooks establish a framework to guide families and staff through how to do specific things and what to expect in specific circumstances. Handbooks are as unique as the staff, families, and communities in which child- and youth-serving programs operate. There is no single right way to create family or staff handbooks. It is, however, a good idea to review your handbooks yearly to determine if revisions are necessary to reflect changes in policy, procedures, activities, or services or to explain things more clearly. Involve your staff in reviewing and making changes to your handbooks. This approach gives you additional eyes and perspectives, so you can make changes that support everyone. As you review both your family and staff handbooks, ask yourself the following questions:

- Do the staff and family handbooks accurately reflect your program's policies and procedures?
- Do both the staff and family handbooks say the same things?

- Do you feel any items need to be added?

- How do families and staff receive the information in your handbooks?

- Are handbooks available to families and staff at all times?

It is also a good idea to make sure that staff and families understand what each policy means. Sharing meaning and expectations helps create an environment where everyone is bound by the same set of rules. One way to do this is to discuss the policies and procedures with staff at a staff meeting. Put staff into groups of two or three people, and ask all the groups to read the same policy or procedure from the staff handbook. Have the groups discuss the meaning of the policy or procedure and then share their conclusions with the whole staff. The whole-group report will tell you whether everyone in the room understands the policy or if you need to reword it for clarity. If it needs rewording, invite staff input to craft a handbook that's easily understood by all.

It is equally important for families to understand the policies and procedures outlined in your family handbook. Often, families receive handbooks only when they enroll their children. An enrollment meeting usually gives little time to reviewing policies and procedures in the handbook. Questions typically lean more toward the cost of care and logistical matters, such as when a child can start the program. But if you establish expectations from the beginning, it'll go a long way toward preventing problems later. Set enrollment appointments for new children so that families realize enrollment is no casual matter. Explain to them how long this meeting will take and what you will be covering during the enrollment meeting. You can give families forms prior to the meeting, and during the meeting you can review both the handbook and the child's paperwork, making sure that the family has provided the appropriate medical, pickup, and contact information. Use a checklist during the enrollment meeting to make sure that you receive all needed information, discuss key policies and procedures, and stay on task.

Several times a year, in your newsletter or at staff or family meetings, highlight policies that have not been followed, that have been reworded, or that have been changed. Have meeting attendees do a scavenger hunt, asking questions related to policies and procedures and using the handbook to find the answers. This activity gets both staff and family members into the handbook and helps them know where to find information when they need it. Start by choosing questions about policies that are most often misunderstood or procedures that are frequently not followed. As you give the answers, you can add relevant comments and then answer questions about the policies and procedures. This process is fun, educational, and nonthreatening, and it avoids being preachy. Participants who get all the answers correct could be entered in a drawing for a gift card for dinner at a local restaurant. Patronizing local restaurants in this way supports the community, and building such relationships can also prompt community businesses to donate items to your program.

Staff and family handbooks should contain all program policies and procedures. (For a list of some common and not-so-common items addressed in family and staff handbooks, please see appendix K.) In an effort to include all possible scenarios, handbooks can become very large and cumbersome. If your handbook is large, you may want to treat it as a resource to consult when people have questions rather than a rulebook that everyone must memorize. Communicate to families and staff that because of the handbook's size, you do not expect them to memorize every policy but instead to refer to the handbook when they are unsure of a policy or procedure. Whenever possible, you should review the most important policies, such as when payments are due, late-payment fees, pickup and drop-off policies, and so on. Some administrators have a "Policy and Procedure" section in their newsletters so they can highlight a few policies and procedures in each issue.

If your handbook is a manageable size, you might send it home with each family and employee. When they are finished reading the handbook, ask them to sign a statement saying that they have read and understood the contents. Keep these statements in the employees' or children's files to be referred to later if needed. Be aware that some family members and employees will sign the sheet without taking time to read the handbook. Decide what will happen to individuals who do not abide by written policies. What is the consequence? Are they removed from the program? The strategies listed in the box below can help you make your handbook helpful and practical.

Tips from the Field

✓ Place a copy of the handbook in a prominent location, so it's handy when staff or families are confused about a policy or procedure.

✓ If you have seasonal policies (such as a written policy for sunscreen use, distributed as needed) that aren't in your handbook, store them in a central location where staff and families can find them easily.

✓ Post your family handbook online.

✓ Help families and staff realize that the handbook is a resource book. They are not expected to memorize it but are expected to refer to it when questions arise.

✓ To help you manage your program's privacy, security, and reputation, consider creating a policy on taking children's pictures or videos with the staff mobile phone and a policy about posting program-centered pictures or information on social media.

Evaluations, Retention, and Dismissals

None of us know all the potentialities that slumber in the spirit of the population, or all the ways in which that population can surprise us when there is the right interplay of events.

VACLAV HAVEL, *DISTURBING THE PEACE*

This chapter discusses the sometimes arduous task of staff evaluation. It also looks at strategies to retain quality staff. Finally, it offers guidance on dismissing staff when necessary, in a fair and legal way. Being prepared and intentionally creating evaluation documents that are unbiased and an environment where staff are valued and can flourish will minimize stress. These practices will also help you build a program where employees love to come to work.

EVALUATIONS

If you've invested time in your staff's job descriptions, training, and handbook, then your employees already know what they are expected to do. However, they may not know how their performance will be evaluated. It's your job to let them know. Give each employee a copy of a blank evaluation form both at orientation and again a few weeks before the evaluation date so there are no misunderstandings about the evaluation criteria. If you do not have a staff evaluation form, you'll find an example in appendix L. Whether you are designing your own evaluation form or using an existing one, make sure you understand the terms used to measure an employee's job performance. Appendix L guides you through the process of creating a program-specific evaluation form and provides you with terms, definitions of the terms, and areas of evaluation based on common job responsibilities. Use what is applicable for your program, and add any new items you feel are needed.

Evaluations are typically done yearly, but they tend to focus on the few months prior to the evaluation. So if an employee did a great project in January and has an evaluation in November, chances are the project is not even mentioned. To make sure you are conducting a fair evaluation, document each person's performance regularly. One way to do so is to divide your staff into four groups. Each month, reflect on how the members of one group have performed. Make a note of things they have done well and things they have struggled with. This reflection does not have to be a long narrative but rather can be a short comment with specific examples. Place these comments in each employee's file. If you use this method, you will end up reflecting on each group three times a year.

In addition to regular reflections on staff performance, it is important to get feedback from your staff on both their peers and themselves. Solicit this feedback in a way that encourages affirmation rather than griping. Ask five questions or fewer. Here are some questions you might ask employees about their coworkers:

- What one thing do you value about your coworker and why?

- What skill does your coworker have that you admire and why?

- Describe a situation in which your coworker went above and beyond.

- In what area could your coworker improve and why?

These open-ended questions ask for specific examples that you could use during the evaluation. They provide only one opportunity to say something negative. The employee being evaluated should also be a part of the feedback process. Here are some questions you might ask employees about themselves:

- What is your favorite thing about your job and why?

- Describe something that happened this past year that made you proud to be working here.

- Describe a situation that you struggled with this year. How did you eventually succeed?

- Name one thing you would like to do next year to enhance your programming.

With all this information, you can provide a well-rounded performance evaluation. Now it is time to schedule a meeting with the employee. Scheduling in advance tells staff that they are important and gives you both time to clear your calendars so you can be engaged in the evaluation and hold the meeting without interruption. During the evaluation, begin with positive feedback and follow up with constructive feedback. Finish the meeting by having the employee help design a professional development plan for the following year. Include as many employee-suggested options as possible. This strategy allows staff to begin taking control of their own professional development.

Tips from the Field

✓ Collect information about staff performance all year long.

✓ Do not wait until evaluations to let staff know they are having problems; address issues as they happen to allow staff to make corrections prior to evaluation.

✓ Write down your comments about performance, and place in the staff files. Do not rely on your memory.

✓ Cite specific examples that illustrate the job skill level of a given situation to help employees understand positive or negative behaviors.

STAFF RETENTION

Every administrator would love to brag about retaining the same staff for multiple years. This is the gold standard that all directors want to achieve. One of the best indicators of an organization's overall health is how long it has retained staff. Losing staff is costly. It takes time and money to replace any individual.

You invest a lot of effort in getting great staff. So how do you make them want to stay? The bottom line is that employees want their efforts to be acknowledged and appreciated. A CEO once said, "If they get their check, and it is for the right amount, what else do they want?" This type of attitude toward staff does not produce a supportive and nurturing workplace. Professionals in the child- and youth-serving world do not expect to become Wall Street millionaires, and you don't have to throw a ticker tape parade each time an employee does a good job, but it's good business sense to make your staff happy whenever you can. You may not be able to offer a large salary, but you can look into benefits that might be appealing, such as a life insurance policy, a 401(k) plan that is available for employee contribution or in conjunction with a small organizational contribution, or a health savings account to offset health-care costs with pretax dollars. You can learn about your options and customize such plans to meet the needs of your organization by contacting an investment broker.

Chapter 8 discussed including staff incentives in your budget. If you have done this, you now have money set aside for saying thank you in little or big ways. There is no need to break the bank. The key to staff retention is keeping morale high by creating a family-like atmosphere that supports all employees. Make your program a fun place to work. Even adults like to play. One organization created a hallway Olympics for its staff during lunchtime and breaktime. The first week offered miniature golf; each employee got three tries to putt a hole in one. The second week offered shuffleboard; employees paired up and kept score all week. At the end of each week, the staff with the highest score got an award. Another organization held an announcement bingo game. All the employees got bingo cards in their mailboxes. Several times a day, a number was drawn and then announced over the PA system. The first employee to get a coverall received a prize. Some other great ways to have fun and build morale are celebrating birthdays and work anniversaries or writing a simple note occasionally to say you noticed what a great job an employee did. Appreciated workers are happy workers. Happy workers like to come to work and go above and beyond in their jobs.

Tips from the Field

✓ Create a four-day workweek to give staff one weekday to run errands and have time for themselves.

✓ Create a substitute staff pool that allows employees to take time off for appointments or family events.

✓ Have fun.

✓ Recognize employees' efforts, and celebrate their successes.

✓ Make employees feel important.

DISMISSALS

Dismissing an employee is something no administrator enjoys. If you need to let someone go for the first time, become familiar with your organization's disciplinary and firing process before you proceed. According to the US Small Business Administration (SBA 2015), "Every state (except Montana) gives employers the option of adopting an 'at-will' employment policy, meaning that an employer may terminate any employee at any time, for any reason or for no reason at all. Sometimes employee agreements or contracts contradict the 'at-will' policy, so check the wording to make sure where you stand." Determine whether your organization has adopted an at-will policy, and make sure your employee policies, procedures, contracts, and employment agreements reflect the at-will policy.

Some organizations have a grievance process. This process provides recourse if employees disagree with their immediate supervisor or feel they have been mistreated in some way. If your organization has a grievance process, become familiar with it, and understand your role in it. Whether your organization has a formal grievance process or not, all dismissals should have several steps so that the employee is aware of an infraction and has time to change the behavior. The process may involve some or all of the following:

- verbal warning
- written warning
- counseling
- time off without pay
- dismissal

You can find a sample job performance warning in appendix M.

Regardless of your organizational process, sometimes an immediate dismissal is in order. Immediate dismissal might be necessary if an employee has endangered someone or committed a crime. Spell out reasons for termination in your staff handbook. Generally, when an incident requiring dismissal occurs, the organization suspends employment immediately, pending the outcome of an investigation. It is also important to know when you cannot dismiss someone. For instance, you cannot dismiss employees based on their age, race, religion, gender, or disability; because they took family or medical leave, military leave, or time off to serve on a jury or vote; or because they are whistleblowers. For more information, visit www.sba.gov/blogs/how-fire-employee-and-stay-within-law.

The first rule of dismissal is to document, document, document—even if your organization is an at-will employer. You should document every event by including a description of the violation, the time and date it occurred, who was present, and what was said. Make note of whether this is a first violation or a subsequent one and what will happen if it occurs again. After you have reviewed the infraction with the employee, have the employee sign a document saying that he or she was informed of the violation and the consequence. Place it in the person's staff file. If the employee commits additional violations, and you have followed all the steps of your organization's dismissal process, and it comes to a point at which you need to let the employee go, call the person into your office along with a witness. Explain why the employee is being fired, and collect any keys, credit cards, or other items that belong to your program. Escort the employee to collect personal belongings and then to the door. Keep all documentation about why you dismissed the individual in case questions arise at a later date.

After an employer dismisses an employee, the employer has some additional responsibilities. There are rules outlining what an employee is legally entitled to when dismissed, such as the continuation of health coverage (COBRA), unemployment insurance, vested retirement, final paycheck, and severance pay.

To gather complete information about dismissing an employee, visit the SBA website at www.sba.gov, the US Equal Employment Opportunity Commission website at www.eeoc.gov/employers, and the US Department of Labor website at www.dol.gov/general/topic/health-plans/cobra.

Tips from the Field

✓ Review your grievance procedures, and make sure they are current.

✓ When you are considering termination, you cannot keep too much documentation.

✓ When employees receive warnings, have them sign and date a document stating that they have received a warning, so that there will be no misunderstanding about whether or when this warning was given.

✓ Remember that a signature on a reprimand does not mean that an employee agrees with the reprimand but rather that they have received it.

✓ Keep documentation of reasons for termination forever.

PART 4

Program Quality Assessment Tools and Operating Requirements

Program assessment tools come in a variety of styles that can address just one aspect of a program or can look at the total program. Individual assessment tools typically look at how the program meets specific criteria within a program area or how the program's policies and procedures create a solid financial and age-appropriate programmatic foundation. Accreditation assessment tools are designed to look at the total program, from administration to family outreach to environmental design to educational opportunities. Each of these types of assessment tools can help programs look objectively at how effectively they operate in a given area or as a whole. Each tool can identify areas of strength and areas that need improvement. By using these types of tools, you can establish a baseline measure of your program's performance and develop ongoing improvement strategies.

Many local, state, and federal regulations can affect how you run your program. Local regulations include rules about zoning, fire, health, and safety. State laws may govern what education your employees need and how many children you can enroll per teacher. Federal laws such as the Americans with Disabilities Act (ADA) and antidiscrimination laws can have an impact on your environment's design and how you hire staff. You should take all these regulations seriously. It is better to conform to these requirements proactively than to find your program in trouble and scramble for solutions.

Part of operating a child- or youth-serving program is the job of withholding and reporting employee income taxes and filing tax returns for your program. Deducting taxes from employees' paychecks and submitting the monies to the various federal, state, and local government entities can be time-consuming. So can paying your organization's quarterly taxes. Setting up a process that helps you plan and track both types of tax obligations will minimize the overall stress and work involved.

Assessment and Accreditation Tools

The accomplishment of individual and collective purposes in the most fulfilling ways possible will create winning organizations.

CRAIG R. HICKMAN AND MICHAEL A. SILVA, *THE FUTURE 500*

Why should you do program assessments or become accredited? Both types of tools offer you an opportunity to take a new look at your program from the ground up and from the inside out. This process can help you improve your program quality and reap other benefits, too.

Some programs become accredited because their state offers a higher federal child care subsidy reimbursement rating for accredited programs. Other programs do so because accreditation allows them to move up more quickly in their state QRIS. Still others are required by their funders to be accredited in order to continue receiving funds. Some programs look to accreditation to unify staff, family, and community efforts to create high-quality care for the community's children. Regardless of why a program chooses to become accredited or to use the self-study associated with accreditation, the process encourages staff to look at high-quality programming as the only way to conduct business.

An accrediting body is an organization that documents whether a program has met a set of prescribed standards. An assessment in the form of a self-study is part of many accreditation processes. Going through an accreditation process can be rewarding for children, families, and staff. It is important to remember accreditation is a journey and not a destination. The process of observations, self-study, or formal assessment should be ongoing so that as staff changes and new children and families enter the program, the needs of the children, families, and staff continue to be met in accordance with accreditation standards.

Accreditation processes vary greatly in price and process from organization to organization. Be aware that not all national accreditations are recognized by all states. Once you have researched the options available for your state, you can make a decision about whether accreditation is right for your program.

In addition to accreditation self-study materials, there are many other formal assessments that child- and youth-serving programs can use to examine and improve their quality and outcomes. Some assessments look at an entire program, while others look at specific areas of a program. This chapter reviews a few of these assessments. It is not meant to be an exhaustive list. The National Center on Child Care Quality Improvement, a division of the US Department of Health and Human Services Office of Child Care, provides an extensive and regularly updated list of assessment tools. For more information, download the list at https://qrisguide.acf.hhs.gov/files/Program_Assessment.pdf. First, let's look at tools that assess an entire program.

A Program Assessment System (APAS)

www.niost.org

APAS was developed by the National Institute of Out-of-School Time (NIOST). This program assessment has three measurement tools: the Survey of Academic and Youth Outcomes (SAYO Staff and Teacher), completed by staff and teachers; the Survey of Academic and Youth Outcomes (SAYO-Youth), completed by youth; and the Assessment of Program Practices Tool (APT)–Observation and Questionnaire. You can use these tools together or separately, depending on the specific needs of your program. This evaluation system is aimed at improving program quality and youth outcomes in after-school programs.

Business Administration Scale for Family Child Care (BAS)

http://mccormickcenter.nl.edu/program-evaluation
/business-administration-scale-bas/

The BAS is designed for family child care providers and is used to look at all aspects of the family child care home. This tool can be used in some state QRISs to determine the overall quality of a program and its business practices. It measures quality on a seven-point scoring scale that examines ten items:

- qualifications and professional development
- income and benefits
- work environment

- fiscal management
- record keeping
- risk management
- provider-parent communication
- community resources
- marketing and public relations
- provider as employer

Council on Accreditation (COA) Standards

http://coanet.org/accreditation/child-and-youth-development
-program-accreditation/

The COA standards were formulated from the National AfterSchool Association's Quality Program Standards. COA's eighth-edition standards include ten additional administrative standards. The standards were wordsmithed to meet the graphic and written standards for the COA system. This accreditation tool is designed for programs that serve school-age children and youth. This system provides a variety of support documents that guide you through the accreditation process, from a self-study to a desk review of policies and procedures, as well as surveys and program observations. All accreditation documents and supporting documents are submitted online. The accreditation standards are divided into three sections:

- after-school program administration
- after-school human resources
- after-school programming and services

Environment Rating Scales

http://ers.fpg.unc.edu

The Environment Rating Scales were developed at the University of North Carolina at Chapel Hill. The scales are four separate assessment tools: the Early Childhood Environment Rating Scale–Revised (ECERS–R), the Infant/Toddler Environment Rating Scale–Revised (ITERS–R), the Family Child Care Environment Rating Scale–Revised (FCCERS–R), and the School-Age Care Environment Rating Scale (SACERS–R). Each of these tools is designed to assess a specific age group or type of group setting. While each tool assesses a different audience and the items assessed vary by tool, the scoring and overall format are the same for all the tools. Some of these tools have supplementary items for programs enrolling children with disabilities. You can use these evaluation tools to determine your program's strengths and weaknesses either in a specific area or as a total program. The tools come with definitions of various terms as well as directions for scoring.

Youth Program Quality Assessment (Youth PQA)

http://etools.highscope.org/pdf/YouthPQA.pdf

The Youth PQA is a research-based instrument. It was designed to evaluate the quality of youth programs and identify staff development needs for structured programs serving grades four through twelve. It is intended to assess the quality of youth programs for the purposes of accountability, evaluation, and program improvement. The instrument has been used in a wide variety of settings, including school-age, community-based, camp, drop-in, and peer or adult mentoring programs. The Youth PQA is a dual-purpose instrument, robust enough to use for high-stakes accountability and research purposes, and user-friendly enough to be used for program self-assessment. It is both an evaluation tool and a learning tool assessing the following areas:

- engagement
- interactions
- professional learning community

- safe environment
- supportive environment
- youth voice and governance

Preschool Program Quality Assessment (Preschool PQA)

www.highscope.org/Content.asp?ContentId=116

This assessment tool for center-based preschool programs examines the following:

- the program learning environment
- interactions
- lesson planning
- family involvement

- staff qualifications
- ongoing professional development for staff
- routine
- organizational management

National Association for the Education of Young Children (NAEYC) Accreditation

www.naeyc.org/academy

NAEYC accreditation is built on a four-step process designed to increase the accountability of the system for children and families. These steps involve enrolling in self-study, becoming an applicant, becoming a candidate, and meeting and maintaining the standards. All indicators fall under the following standards:

- building positive relationships
- curriculum
- teaching
- assessment of child progress
- health

- teachers
- families
- community relationships
- physical environment
- leadership and management

National Early Childhood Program Accreditation (NECPA)

www.necpa.net

NECPA accredits licensed programs serving primarily preschool children. It will include school-age programs that are a component of a center-based program provided that the majority of children in the school-age program are eight years old or younger. NECPA accreditation assesses the following areas:

- adult and child interaction
- staff framing
- health and safety
- physical environment
- administration
- parent and community relationships

Program Administration Scale (PAS), Second Edition

http://mccormickcenter.nl.edu/program-administration-scale-pas-2nd-ed/

The PAS assessment tool is administered by the director of an early care and education program to review its administrative practices and outline strengths and areas for improvement. PAS measures the following:

- human resource development
- personnel cost and allocation
- center operations
- child assessment
- fiscal management
- program planning and evaluation
- family partnerships
- marketing and public relations
- technology
- staff qualifications

Quality Assurance System (QAS)

http://qas.foundationsinc.org/start.asp?st=1

QAS was developed to help after-school programs conduct quality assessment and continuous improvement planning. It is an online tool designed to be general enough for use in a range of school- and community-based programs serving children in kindergarten through grade twelve. It focuses on quality at the site level. Programs using the QAS start with an initial assessment from which observers identify areas of strength as well as those that need improvement. Once the assessment is finished, the tool helps programs develop specific improvement strategies. QAS is meant to be conducted once at the beginning of the program year and again midway through the year. The tool is based on seven building blocks:

- program planning and improvement
- leadership
- facility and program space
- health and safety
- staffing
- family and community connections
- social climate

The final two assessment tools look at literacy and language development in family child care homes, centers, and school-based programs serving kindergarten through grade three. They explore how literacy is being taught and encouraged within each of these settings.

Child/Home Early Language and Literacy Observation (CHELLO)

www.brookespublishing.com/resource-center/screening-and-assessment/chello

Early Language and Literacy Classroom Observation (ELLCO)

www.brookespublishing.com/resource-center/screening-and-assessment/ellco
The purpose of these assessment tools is to measure the quality of the language and literacy environment in a family child care home, preschool, and kindergarten through third grade. These tools focus on the importance of preliteracy and literacy activities within the early childhood and education setting. They examine the care provider's methods, materials, and interactions within the environment and outline targeted interventions.

Tips from the Field

✓ Do your research, and find an accreditation process that fits your program.

✓ Accreditation is a walk on a path and not a destination; as staff change and new children enter the program, changes may need to happen to meet the needs of the staff and children as well as to meet the accreditation standards.

✓ Before choosing an accrediting organization, review the accreditation standards to make sure your program can financially manage the changes needed to meet the standards.

✓ Even if you do not decide to become accredited, use the accreditation self-study processes to help you outline areas of strength and areas that need improvement.

✓ Assessment tools are a great way to get staff on the same page about job expectations.

✓ Accreditation is for ongoing, everyday operation, not just for the site visit. If you're changing your program only for the site visit, the children will let the observer know that "we have not been able to do this before" or "this is a new game" or "we have never had this snack before."

Inspections

I am always ready to learn, although I do not always like being taught.

WINSTON CHURCHILL, SPEECH TO THE HOUSE OF COMMONS

A child- or youth-serving program needs many different kinds of inspections. Each inspection looks at a different aspect of the program. Inspections are designed to assess the overall safety of the program's space, the quality of care, and the processes in place for emergencies. The agencies and organizations that conduct these inspections can provide a wealth of information and be helpful resources for your program. So approach inspections as learning experiences, and take the inspectors up on their suggestions.

BUILDING, HEALTH, AND FIRE INSPECTIONS

All child- and youth-serving programs undergo building, health, and fire inspections. Yearly inspections of buildings, kitchens, and fire safety are standard for most communities. You will need to check with your local building department to see what building codes apply and what types of inspections are required in your area for child- and youth-serving programs. Be aware that most communities charge fees for inspections, so make sure to budget for these.

The US Department of Labor's Occupational Safety and Health Administration (OSHA) website, located at www.osha.gov, provides guidance on many safety issues, including fire safety. It outlines employer responsibilities, how to place and use portable fire extinguishers and fire detection systems (smoke and carbon monoxide detectors and sprinkler systems), and how to develop an evacuation plan. It also offers a downloadable checklist for developing and implementing an emergency action plan (EAP). Once you have your EAP in place and have developed a system to document fire drills and other emergency drills, you will need to train staff for these drills. Most licensing agencies require child- and youth-serving programs to hold fire drills and other safety drills as well as to keep records of when these drills were held. Your local fire department may be able to help you with drills, set up times to check your smoke and carbon monoxide detectors, and connect you with qualified people to check and replace your fire extinguishers.

Your local health department can give you guidelines and regulations for operating a kitchen that prepares and serves meals for staff and children in your care. Guidelines address issues such as specific temperatures for serving food and for storing food in the refrigerator and freezer, procedures for preparing food and sanitizing cooking and serving surfaces, and more. Usually individuals who work in the kitchen must take a mandatory training class. Kitchen inspections happen at regular intervals throughout the year. Once you have received a certificate allowing you to cook and serve food within your program, you need to post that certificate in the kitchen area. Some organizations make a copy of the certificate and store the original certificate in the administrative office for safekeeping.

Tips from the Field

✔ Review all existing inspections to find out if anything needed to be fixed, and determine whether it was indeed fixed.

✔ Conduct periodic inspections yourself to see if you need to schedule safety training and if evacuation diagrams are posted properly.

✔ Review your program's safety drills (fire, tornado, earthquake, shelter in place, and lockdown or active shooter drills) with staff quarterly.

✔ Update your safety drills tracking sheet the day you conduct them, and make sure to include the time conducted.

✔ Replace smoke and carbon monoxide detector batteries yearly. Note the date when you replace them. Mark on your calendar the date when they need to be changed again. October is Fire Prevention Month—a great time to check units and change batteries.

ADA ACCESSIBILITY REQUIREMENTS

Since passage of the Americans with Disabilities Act (ADA) in 1990, federal laws have governed accessibility issues for anyone with a temporary or permanent disability. Titles II and III of the ADA and Section 504 of the Rehabilitation Act of 1973 set mandatory guidelines for group care settings that enroll children with special needs—those who have physical, psychological, or cognitive disabilities. This includes all child- and youth-serving programs.

By law, all child- and youth-serving programs must be inclusive and must allow enrollment of children with special needs. According to the ADA, a team that includes the child's parents or guardians, school and medical personnel, and other individuals working directly with the child (such as school-age program staff) makes the final determination about placement for a child with special needs. If the needs of a child cannot be met in the program in which the child is enrolled, if the child poses a risk of harm to the health or safety of others, or if the child's care would fundamentally alter the nature of the program, alternate programming should be considered to ensure the child's safety, well-being, and overall development.

While staff are responsible for ensuring that all children's needs are met in the program space, site administrators must determine how to create a safe and successful environment for children with special needs. By law, these children must have equal opportunity to be enrolled and then freely participate in your program. You may not have a child with special needs now, but all child- and youth-serving programs have a legal obligation to make reasonable environmental modifications or accommodations if a child with special needs should enroll or if a child currently in your program acquires a temporary disability, such as a broken leg. Children who have asthma or severe allergies also are supported by the ADA. They may need reasonable accommodations, and staff may need training to give medicine appropriately. Reasonable modifications or accommodations means making changes needed to help children with special needs reach their potential. Many of these modifications can be carried out without much difficulty or expense. For example, simple and inexpensive changes include the following:

- Add ramps or handrails to help a child with limited mobility.

- Install grab bars in the bathroom.

- Obtain large-piece puzzles for a child with limited fine-motor skills.

- Purchase or borrow large-print books for a child with limited eyesight from the library or your local Association for the Blind and Visually Impaired.

- Rearrange furniture to create a space for wheelchairs and walkers at lunch, sensory, and activity tables.

- Rearrange furniture to create wider pathways to accommodate walkers and wheelchairs.

You should not simply assume that your facility cannot accommodate a child who has a disability without major and costly changes. As you research ADA compliance for your program, know that tax deductions are available for small businesses to offset the cost of making changes needed to comply with the ADA. Consult with your tax advisor or the Internal Revenue Service (IRS) to learn more. Also, you can get assistance in interpreting ADA guidelines free of charge by visiting the US Department of Justice Civil Rights Division website at www.ada.gov or by calling 800-514-0301.

Tips from the Field

✔ Determine whether your building is ADA accessible.

✔ If you're in doubt about ADA compliance, ask questions.

✔ Reach out to community agencies that serve children with disabilities and see what equipment and services you can tap into for your program.

LICENSING REQUIREMENTS

Even if you have been a director in a child- or youth-serving organization before taking your current job, it is important that you learn what the most up-to-date licensing requirements are and what responsibility you have for implementing them. Never assume that you already know what to do, or that a previous administrator was in complete compliance. Obtain licensing requirements from the appropriate licensing agency in your community. This agency will outline expectations for program space, activities, staff education, and administrative policies and practices. Take time to review the latest version of the licensing requirements. Highlight everything you understand and know you're complying with in green and things you are unsure of or have questions about in yellow. Once you have clarified and complied with the yellow items, highlight over them with blue to change them to green. When you complete this process, you will have a good understanding of licensing requirements and will know what you need to do to stay in compliance.

Licensing requirements vary from state to state and from community to community. Many states define the types of programs that require licensure. Not all states require all child- and youth-serving programs to be licensed, or they may have an age limit, such as fourteen or sixteen years, for required licensing. Some states include school-age licensure within their early childhood rules. Other states have a specific set of regulations for each specific type of program. It's important to understand these regulations before you begin planning or redesigning your space, so you don't end up having to redo this work. Even if you are not required to go through a licensure process, make sure you have clear evidence of the following:

- facility and grounds that protect children from harm

- staff who are responsible, caring, and well-trained

- staff who have not been convicted of a felony or child-related misdemeanor

- program goals that reflect an understanding of how children grow and learn

- program activities and space that meet the needs of all the children served

Tips from the Field

✓ Find out what inspections are required by your local, state, and federal government.

✓ Reach out to the local inspectors for resources to help you maintain compliance.

✓ Document all safety drills, and include date, time, and who was involved.

✓ Make sure that safety training is part of the yearly training of staff.

✓ Mark the date of purchase on all smoke, fire, and carbon monoxide detectors.

✓ Train staff on all children's disabilities and how to support them appropriately.

✓ Train staff on the proper use of an epinephrine injector (EpiPen), a glucometer, an inhaler, a nebulizer, and other medical devices.

Income Taxes and Payroll Deductions

Taxes, after all, are the dues that we pay for the privileges of membership in an organized society.

FRANKLIN D. ROOSEVELT, CAMPAIGN SPEECH IN WORCESTER, MASSACHUSETTS

While you may not be the person in your organization who handles employee income tax and other payroll deductions, their payments to the proper organizations, or the filing of state, local, and federal income taxes for your organization, you will still play a role in this process. Your organization has two main types of income tax responsibilities. One responsibility is the payment of your organization's income taxes (if applicable—nonprofit organizations may be exempt from income taxation). The other responsibility is the withholding of employees' income taxes from their paychecks. In addition to the mandated deduction, your organization may withhold additional deductions from an employee's wages that are specific to your organization. It is important for you to educate yourself on the types of taxes, their payment requirements, and other deductions your organization makes available to employees.

ORGANIZATIONAL INCOME TAXES

Regardless of the type of care your organization provides, the organization's income after allowable deductions (net income) is taxable unless you are a qualifying nonprofit organization. If you are a nonprofit organization, you may still be required to file an Annual Exempt Organization Return. It is always best to discuss your responsibility for filing the organizational income tax with a CPA or check with the IRS. The IRS has many online resources and booklets to guide you in preparing the required tax forms.

It is important to know what expenses you can and cannot deduct on your income tax return. When you're determining your net income, you will not only need to know what you can deduct but also need to track these expenses throughout the year. Assuming that you are reviewing your organization's revenues and expenditures regularly, as described in chapters 8 and 9, you should already have a handle on what your organization has spent in each budgetary line item. If you have a CPA on staff or on contract to prepare your organization's tax return, the CPA will be able to provide a complete list of deductible expenses. Meet with the CPA shortly after beginning your new job, and review the list of deductions to make sure you are entering them correctly and that you have a way to break them out of the budget. If you do not have a CPA, you can obtain Publication 535 from the IRS. This publication explains what you can and cannot deduct. You can find it online at www.irs.gov/uac/about-publication-535. The IRS website can also provide you with other forms and publications that explain all the aspects of income tax filing and payments at www.irs.gov.

Tips from the Field

✓ When in doubt, ask questions.

✓ Doing a monthly or quarterly tabulation of your allowable deductions makes quick work of preparing your tax return.

✓ Make sure all your expense receipts are filed under the appropriate deduction.

✓ Scanning receipts avoids the problem of faded paper receipts.

✓ Ask your CPA how long the tax materials need to be kept for your specific organization.

✓ Do not forget that some communities require businesses to pay income taxes.

Even if your organization is a nonprofit, it may still have some filing requirements. It is important that you are aware of the regulations that apply to your specific nonprofit status. The IRS website provides many resources for nonprofit organizations, such as annual reporting and filing information and educational resources and guidance documents. For these resources and more, visit www .irs.gov/charities-non-profits.

You will also need to contact your state revenue department to determine whether you need to file state income taxes, as some states do not have state income taxes. In addition, many local communities also have income taxes. It is important that you do your research, because ignorance of tax laws will not protect you if you run afoul of them. Federal income tax returns are due on April 15 each year, but state and local tax return deadlines may vary.

EMPLOYEE INCOME TAXES AND OTHER PAYROLL DEDUCTIONS

As chapter 8 discusses, it's important to keep track of employees' income tax withholdings and submit the right sums to the right agencies at the right time. If you are the one handling employee income taxes, be sure to review IRS Publication 15 (Circular E), the Employer's Tax Guide, at www.irs.gov/uac/about -publication-15. This document explains your tax responsibilities as an employer.

Your organization, as an employer, is required by the government to withhold certain payroll taxes and to submit the withheld taxes to the proper governmental agency in a timely manner using a variety of tax-related forms. Some of these are IRS forms W-2, W-3, 941, and 1099. A W-2 shows the amount of taxes withheld from an employee's paycheck for the year. You must file a W-2 form for each person employed by your organization during the previous year (even if you don't currently employ that person) who received six hundred dollars or more in remunerations. You must file W-2s no later than January 31, accompanied by W-3s (Transmittal of Wage and Tax Statements). Employers who withhold income taxes, social security tax, or Medicare tax from employees' paychecks or who must pay the employer's portion of social security or Medicare tax use Form 941 to report those taxes. This form needs to be filed quarterly. Form 1099 is used to document various types of income other than wages, salaries, and tips that your organization has paid to individuals during the year. The deadline for filing 1099s is usually at the end of February but changes from year to year, so be sure to consult the IRS website at www.irs.gov/uac/about-form-1099misc for current information.

Employers often deduct more from employee paychecks than government-mandated taxes. Your organization might make additional payroll deductions for the following items:

- health insurance
- vision insurance
- dental insurance
- long-term and short-term disability
- life insurance
- retirement plan
- child support
- child care
- union dues
- wage garnishment

Allowing employees to have such items deducted from their wages does come with an organizational cost. When an employer makes these payroll deductions, the employer is responsible for paying the appropriate recipients on behalf of employees. It will take someone's time to make sure deductions are correct and paid to the appropriate recipients at the correct time. The more staff you have, the more time it takes. So make sure this time is figured into job descriptions and budgets.

If your organization allows nontax payroll deductions, then provide employees with a voluntary deduction sheet that shows what can be deducted and the amount of each deduction. For instance, if the program offers all the deductions listed above, and an employee wants to opt in only for the health insurance and long-term disability insurance, the employee should sign a release stating the amount for each item and that the employee asked for these payroll deductions. This makes employees aware of what will be deducted so there are no surprises when they receive their first check. It is a good idea to add an "other" line to the list of available payroll deductions so your form will be usable if a new option becomes available. The "other" category also allows customization for each employee. For an example of a payroll deduction authorization form, see appendix N.

Tips from the Field

✓ Maintain a file with tax forms that you use regularly.

✓ Make sure to check the IRS website often, as federal tax law changes frequently.

✓ Always get in writing what employees want deducted from their paychecks.

✓ You must always comply with a court-ordered wage garnishment.

✓ Stay on top of payroll deductions and payments to the appropriate organizations; your employees depend on you to make them on time.

Job Descriptions and Statement of Commitment

PRCC CHILD DEVELOPMENT CENTER

Job Description: Center Administrator

Basic Function:

- Responsible for the day-to-day operation of PRCC in a fiscally responsible manner. Provides high-quality day care for children by cooperating with PRCC Child Development Center's board of directors in planning and evaluating program, supervising center staff, and interacting with parents and the community.

Characteristic Duties:

- Plan, organize, and administer Child Development Center program.
- Work with licensing personnel, board members, center staff, and community in ongoing improvements of the Child Development Center.
- Correspond with the board of directors.
- Attend and participate in professional meetings and conferences.
- Maintain ongoing financial records and the status of taxes, licenses, and other commitments.
- Work to obtain grants and other funds to meet long-range goals of Child Development Center.
- Supervise fiscal, purchasing, and other business management activities.
- Coordinate equipment maintenance and repair.
- Administrate in accordance with board policy and budget regarding day care staff: recruit, hire and/or dismiss, orient, supervise, and evaluate activities.
- Schedule staff appropriately to meet licensure requirements.
- Supervise, review, and help teachers plan, organize, and supervise activities designed to meet physical, emotional, and creative needs of the children and to assure their care and protection.
- Observe and participate in program activities. Plan and administer program evaluations.
- Plan and schedule staff meetings and in-service training programs.
- Institute and administer ongoing program of public relations to recruit clients.
- Schedule and oversee interviewing of new children and their parents.
- Contract with clients for service.
- Plan and schedule parent-staff meetings.
- Plan, organize, supervise, and administer a program of parent education and encourage parent participation in existing community programs.
- Supervise parent volunteer program.

Supervision:

- Supervised by the board of directors.

Qualifications:

- Has bachelor's degree in early childhood education or related field of study, as specified by the State of Ohio licensing codes.
- Is experienced in licensed day care.
- Must demonstrate supervisory ability (references, past work experience, interview questions).
- Has working knowledge of various community cultures, as they may affect children served by the Child Development Center (references, past work experience, interview questions).
- Must pass required physical examination.

Requirement for All Child Day Care Workers:

- Police background check and fingerprint record.

If Employed by PRCC Child Development Center, Must Learn Center Policies and Procedures in Regard to:

- Communicable disease and exclusion of sick children.
- First aid and medical emergency.
- Fire evacuation.
- Tornado and severe weather evacuation.
- Child abuse reporting.
- Discipline.
- Cause(s) for termination.

PRCC CHILD DEVELOPMENT CENTER

Job Description: Administrative Office Coordinator

Basic Function:

- Assists administrator with the day-to-day operations for PRCC and maintains basic office management responsibilities.

Duties:

- Assists administrator in office: phones, communicating with parents, and so on.
- Assumes center responsibilities in the administrator's absence.
- Monitors and submits office, teacher, and cleaning supply orders.
- Opens and closes center as indicated by administrator.
- Reports problems or concerns with children or parents to the administrator.
- Actively participates in regular staff meetings, parent meetings, and workshops.
- Teaches segments of program as required by plan; helping in rooms as needed.
- Assists teachers in obtaining room supplies such as copies, forms, and so on.
- Schedules and implements monthly fire drill and ensures all staff are familiar with procedures.
- Assists administrator in maintaining center records ensuring compliance with licensure requirements.

Financial Records

- Maintains record of tuition paid and sick and vacation days used for each family.
- Submits financial statements to families as requested or needed.
- Submits reports of weekly or monthly income to administrator and board of directors as requested.
- Tracks and maintains Hamilton County Department of Job and Family Services (HCDJFS) / Butler County Department of Job and Family Services (BCDJFS) attendance records and submits biweekly or monthly vouchers for payment.

Children's Records

- Maintains emergency transportation forms.
- Maintains children's medical forms.
- Maintains and updates weekly attendance and monthly rosters.

Employee Records

- Prepares and coordinates work schedules.
- Documents days off and helps arrange substitute staff for absentees.
- Tracks teachers' attendance and punctuality; monitors overtime hours.
- Tracks total hours worked to determine vacation days.
- Ensures center's compliance with licensure requirements.

Supervision:

- Supervised and evaluated by administrator.

Qualifications:

- Has recent experience in early childhood setting, experience in licensed daycare, and at least forty in-service training hours.
- Has strong background in bookkeeping.
- References of past experience must demonstrate supervisory abilities.
- Must pass required physical.

Requirement for All Child Day Care Workers:

- Police background check and fingerprint record.

If Employed by PRCC Child Development Center, Must Learn Center Policies and Procedures in Regard to:

- Communicable disease and exclusion of sick children.
- First aid and medical emergency.
- Fire evacuation.
- Tornado and severe weather evacuation.
- Child abuse reporting.
- Discipline.
- Cause(s) for termination.

PRCC CHILD DEVELOPMENT CENTER

Job Description: Lead Teacher

Basic Function:

- Teaches class and carries out a daily program to meet the physical and developmental needs of children.

Duties:

- Plans teaching activities and daily schedule to address all children's needs.
- Teaches program as required by plan.
- Lesson plans are to be turned in on Friday p.m. for the next week.
- All supplies are to be in place for Monday morning.
- All prep (cutting, copying, and so on) is to be done by Friday afternoon.
- Any supplies needed should be requested by Wednesday (to be purchased by administrator before Friday).
- Actively participates in regular staff meetings, parent meetings, and workshops.
- Required to attend in-service training.
- Keep progress evaluation for each child. Coordinates parent-teacher conferences twice a year.
- Reports problems with children or parents to administrator.
- Acquires familiarity with licensure requirements. Ensures Child Development Center's compliance with requirements at all times.
- Maintains center files and records related to teaching and to teacher's own room.
- Maintains attendance records for the days of the week.
- Maintains cleanliness of room and all areas of center as they are used.
- Keeps playground area presentable.
- Removes broken toys and reports to administrator anything that is unsafe.
- Works in cooperation with other staff.

Supervision:

- Supervised and evaluated by the administrator. The board of directors' president approves final hiring/termination.
- Jointly coordinates any student teaching with the administrator.

Qualifications:

- Has bachelor's or associate's degree in early childhood education. Child development associate (CDA) will be acceptable if employee has long-term, recent experience in comparable position.
- Must demonstrate supervisory experience.
- Must pass required physical examination.

Requirement for All Child Day Care Workers:

- Police background check and fingerprint record.

If Employed by PRCC Child Development Center, Must Learn Center Policies and Procedures in Regard to:

- Communicable disease and exclusion of sick children.
- First aid and medical emergency.
- Fire evacuation.
- Tornado and severe weather evacuation.
- Child abuse reporting.
- Discipline.
- Cause(s) for termination.

PRCC CHILD DEVELOPMENT CENTER

Job Description: Assistant Teacher

Basic Function:

- Assists the lead teacher in the classroom and carries out a daily program to meet physical and developmental needs of children. Receives supervision from the lead teacher and center administrator.

Characteristic Duties:

- Assists the lead teacher in the classroom as directed in providing care and protection for assigned children.
- Supervises children's play activities.
- Participates in group games.
- Enforces safety rules.
- Encourages children's social interaction.
- Participates in staff meetings, training sessions, conferences, and workshops.
- Attends and participates in parent group meetings.
- Arranges environment and prepares supplies, making sure both are accessible and in good condition.
- Performs related duties as assigned.

Qualifications:

- Has high school diploma.
- Has previous classroom experience and knowledge of preschool teaching activity methods and materials.

Requirement for All Child Day Care Workers:

- Police background check and fingerprint record.

If Employed by PRCC Child Development Center,
Must Learn Center Policies and Procedures in Regard to:

- Communicable disease and exclusion of sick children.
- First aid and medical emergency.
- Fire evacuation.
- Tornado and severe weather evacuation.
- Child abuse reporting.
- Discipline.
- Cause(s) for termination.

My Expectations for You as an Employee of Pleasant Run Church of Christ Child Development Center:

- Be in your room ready to care for children at your start time. (This may require you to arrive earlier to take care of any personal, non-job-related business or for dropping your children off in their rooms and getting them signed in and set for the day.)
- Arrive properly groomed and dressed for the day. (Please refer to handbook page 7 for dress code.)
- Do the required daily chores on your cleaning list and turn it in at the end of the week.
- Make sure all parent letters and information get sent home in a timely manner and that parents have signed that they received the same information.
- Make sure all children in your care are signed in with the proper arrival and departure times.
- Prepare daily sheets for each child as requested by their parents.
- If children depart early, let Peggy know so that we can use the time efficiently. It is everyone's job to hold down labor costs for the good of the center.
- If you must make an appointment on a scheduled workday, do your best to make it during your breaktime so that there are enough teachers here for the children.
- If you are a closer, it is your job to make sure the playground is straightened before you leave.
- Turn in your supply request list at the end of the week so that you can start your following week with everything you need. If you will need milk or juice, write it on the board in the office. Do not leave your room to get supplies.
- Use your cell phone only outside your room when you can do so and leave the classroom in ratio. (Please refer to handbook page 11.)
- Attend all staff meetings.
- Participate in all day care–related special events.
- Attend all required classes that are scheduled for you.

PRCC CHILD DEVELOPMENT CENTER

Statement of Commitment

As an individual who works with young children, I commit myself to furthering the values of early childhood education as they are reflected in the National Association for the Education of Young Children (NAEYC) Code of Ethical Conduct.

To the best of my ability I will:

- Ensure that programs for young children are based on current knowledge of child development and early childhood education.
- Respect and support families in their task of nurturing children.
- Respect colleagues in early childhood education and support them in maintaining the NAEYC Code of Ethical Conduct.
- Serve as an advocate for children, their families, and their teachers in community and society.
- Maintain high standards of professional conduct.
- Recognize how personal values, opinions, and biases can affect professional judgment.
- Be open to new ideas and be willing to learn from the suggestions of others.
- Continue to learn, grow, and contribute as a professional.
- Honor the ideals and principles of the NAEYC Code of Ethical Conduct.

This Statement of Commitment expresses those basic personal commitments that individuals must make in order to align themselves with the profession's responsibilities as set forth in the NAEYC Code of Ethical Conduct.

Family Year-End Tax Statement

(program name)
(program address)
(program phone number)

(Year) Child Care Yearly Payment Statement

For: _____

_____

_____

(parent's or guardian's name and address)

Child care was provided for: _____
(child or children's name or names)

From: _____ **Through:** _____
(date)   *(date)*

Total amount paid for services in (year): _____
$ *(dollar amount)*

Signature of provider: _____
(director's signature)

Provider's tax ID or SSN: _____
(tax ID or SSN)

Signature of parent or guardian: _____
(parent's or guardian's signature)

Date: _____
(date of signing)

Sample Work Grid

Daily	Weekly	Monthly	Quarterly	Semiannually	Yearly
Collect attendance.	Review time sheets and get information to accounting to generate paychecks.	Enter fees paid per child into tracking system.	Meet with accountant to review your expenditures and revenue to date.	Meet with accountant to determine the need for budget reallocation based on expenditures and revenue to date.	Review handbooks.
Collect lunch count.		Determine staff professional development needs and schedule development opportunities.	Pay quarterly taxes, social security, and workers' compensation.		Review job descriptions.
Enter food program information.	Review budget.				Create family tax statements.
Conduct one-on-one meetings with staff (1/5 of staff per day).	Order food.	Conduct staff evaluations on the anniversary of each employee's hire date.		Determine marketing efforts for the next six months.	Create proposed budget for next year.
Allot time for one tour or orientation per day.	Enter weekly attendance for children receiving child care subsidy.	Attend community meetings.		Plan a family meeting.	Review marketing materials and update if needed.
Do classroom walk-through.	Order supplies.	Meet with cook to review or create lunch menu for following month.		Plan parent-staff conferences.	Conduct a day of training or team building for all staff.
	Enter children receiving meals through CACFP into data system.	Pay benefit premiums (health care insurance, etc.).		Review staff job application form.	
	Review lesson plans for next week.	File food program paperwork.		Review staff orientation plan.	
	Conduct staff meeting.	File child care subsidy paperwork.			
	Conduct one classroom observation.				
	Contact families who are behind in payment of fees.				

Sample Program Budget

	Budget	Year to date	Jan.	Feb.	Mar.	Apr.	May	Jun.	Jul.	Aug.	Sep.	Oct.	Nov.	Dec.
REVENUE														
2000 Fees														
2001 Part-time														
2002 Full-time														
2003 School-age														
2004 Camp program														
2010 Grants														
2010 Clay Foundation														
2011 City Foundation														
2020 QRIS														
2021 Yearly stipend														
2030 Child care subsidy														
2031 Monthly reimbursement														
2040 Food program (CACFP)														
2041 Monthly reimbursement														
2050 Investment income														
2051 Banking interest (checking, savings)														
2052 CDs, bonds, stocks														

	Budget	Year to date	Jan.	Feb.	Mar.	Apr.	May	Jun.	Jul.	Aug.	Sep.	Oct.	Nov.	Dec.
EXPENDITURES														
3000 Staffing														
3001 Base pay														
3002 Federal, state, & local taxes, social security, Medicare														
3003 Workers' compensation														
3004 Benefits														
3005 Staff incentives														
3006 Background checks														
3007 Orientation														
3008 Professional organization membership dues														
3009 Professional development														
3010 Substitutes														
3011 Building														
3012 Mortgage or rent														
3013 Utilities														
3014 Security														
3015 Maintenance														
3016 Cleaning services														
3017 Lawn care														
3018 Snow removal														
3019 Inspection fees														
3020 Equipment														
3021 Computer & Internet														
3022 Phone														

	Budget	Year to date	Jan.	Feb.	Mar.	Apr.	May	Jun.	Jul.	Aug.	Sep.	Oct.	Nov.	Dec.
3023 Copier & printer														
3024 Copier & printer maintenance														
3025 Refrigeration														
3030 Office supplies														
3031 Paper														
3032 Toner														
3033 Postage														
3034 Credit card processing														
3035 Marketing materials														
3036 Bank fees & checks														
3037 Miscellaneous														
3040/3050 Program Materials														
3041 Chairs														
3042 Cribs														
3043 Crib mattresses														
3044 High chairs														
3045 Storage cabinets														
3046 Shelving														
3047 Sensory tables														
3048 Tables														
3049 Refrigerators														
3050 Stoves, ovens														
3051 Microwaves														
3052 Dishwashers														

	Budget	Year to date	Jan.	Feb.	Mar.	Apr.	May	Jun.	Jul.	Aug.	Sep.	Oct.	Nov.	Dec.
3053 Food service contract														
3054 Food														
3055 Consumables														
3060 Learning Materials														
3061 Consumables														
3062 Learning materials														
3063 Books														
3070 Transportation														
3071 Insurance														
3072 Vehicle purchase, rental														
3073 Maintenance														
3074 Staff training & licensing														
3080 Insurance														
3081 Liability														
3082 Building														
3083 Transportation														
3090 Accreditation & certification														
3091 Application fee														
3092 Materials fee														
4000 Capital projects														
4001 Playground improvement														
4002 Kitchen remodel														
4003 HVAC upgrade														
4004 New roof														

Petty Cash Voucher

Voucher # _____

Vendor _____

Items purchased	Cost line item
_____	_____
_____	_____
_____	_____
_____	_____

Bought by _____

Signature _____

Date _____

Reason for using petty cash:

☐ Needed immediately

☐ Not a contracted service

☐ Other

_____

_____

Please attach original receipt to this voucher.

Sample Job Application

Insert your organization's logo, name, address, telephone number, and web address, or use company letterhead that already has this information.

Application for Employment

An equal opportunity employer statement should go here. For example:

(Program name) is an equal opportunity employer and does not discriminate against applicants based on race, color, nation of origin, creed, religion, age, sex, marital status, pregnancy, disability, sexual orientation, sexual preference, disability, or veteran status.

Name _____ **Date** _____

Address _____

_____

Length of residence at the above address _____

If less than 3 years, provide previous address _____

_____

Position applying for
☐ Full-time   ☐ Part-time

Date available _____   **Salary desired** _____

Phone _____   **E-mail** _____

Are you over 18 years old?
☐ Yes   ☐ No

Are you legally eligible for employment in the United States? (If you are offered employment, you will be required to provide documentation to verify eligibility.)
☐ Yes   ☐ No

Education

Please mark education and training that makes you qualified for the position to which you are applying. Mark all that apply. (If you are offered employment, you will be required to provide documentation to verify your education.)

☐ **High school diploma**

☐ **GED**

☐ **CDA**

☐ **Associate's (2-year) degree**

☐ **Bachelor's (4-year) degree**

School attended _____

Dates attended _____

Degree earned _____

Other Education

School _____

City and state _____

Course _____

Certificate earned _____

School _____

City and state _____

Course _____

Certificate earned _____

Training
Please mark all that apply.

First aid and CPR	**Excel**
☐ Yes (date) _____ ☐ No	☐ Yes (date) _____ ☐ No
Communicable disease	**PowerPoint**
☐ Yes (date) _____ ☐ No	☐ Yes (date) _____ ☐ No
Blood-borne pathogens	**Core knowledge**
☐ Yes (date) _____ ☐ No	☐ Yes (date) _____ ☐ No
Bus safety	**Learning domain**
☐ Yes (date) _____ ☐ No	☐ Yes (date) _____ ☐ No
Food service training	**Accreditation**
☐ Yes (date) _____ ☐ No	☐ Yes (date) _____ ☐ No
Accounting software	**QRIS**
☐ Yes (date) _____ ☐ No	☐ Yes (date) _____ ☐ No
Word processing software	**Other** _____
☐ Yes (date) _____ ☐ No	☐ Yes (date) _____ ☐ No

Have you ever been employed in any department or program of *(organization name)* before?
☐ Yes ☐ No

If yes, please describe: _____

_____

Department or program _____

Dates of employment _____

Record of Conviction

During the past 10 years, have you ever been convicted of a crime other than a minor traffic offense?
☐ Yes　　☐ No

If yes, please explain. Give date of conviction, nature of the crime, and any other information you would like to provide. (Be aware that a background check will be done prior to hiring.)

_____

_____

_____

_____

If you are applying for a bus driver position or your position requires you to drive the program bus, you will be required to show proof of a valid driver's license and should explain any moving violations within the past 3 years below.

_____

_____

_____

_____

Employment History

Please list the past 5 employers first, including US military service.

May we contact your present employer?
☐ Yes　　☐ No

If any employment was under a different last name, provide name here.

_____

If a nickname was used during a previous employment, provide that name here.

_____

Employer _____

Address _____

_____

Phone _____ Position _____

Dates of employment _____

Salary _____ Supervisor _____

Duties _____

_____

☐ Full-time   ☐ Part-time

Reason for leaving _____

_____

Employer _____

Address _____

_____

Phone _____ Position _____

Dates of employment _____

Salary _____ Supervisor _____

Duties _____

_____

☐ Full-time   ☐ Part-time

Reason for leaving _____

_____

Employer _____

Address _____

_____

Phone _____ Position _____

Dates of employment _____

Salary _____ Supervisor _____

Duties_____

_____

☐ Full-time   ☐ Part-time

Reason for leaving _____

_____

Employer _____

Address _____

_____

Phone _____ Position _____

Dates of employment _____

Salary _____ Supervisor _____

Duties_____

_____

☐ Full-time   ☐ Part-time

Reason for leaving _____

_____

Employer _____

Address _____

_____

Phone _____   Position _____

Dates of employment _____

Salary _____   Supervisor _____

Duties_____

_____

☐ Full-time   ☐ Part-time

Reason for leaving _____

_____

If there are gaps in work history, please explain them below.

_____

_____

_____

_____

References

Please provide two personal and two professional references below. Please place an asterisk (*) next to the best mode of communication to reach your references.

Professional references:

Name _____

Address _____

_____

Phone _____   E-mail _____

Name _____

Address _____

_____

Phone _____   E-mail _____

Personal references:

Name _____

Address _____

_____

Phone _____   E-mail _____

Name _____

Address _____

_____

Phone _____   E-mail _____

A statement for the applicant to sign that outlines the authenticity of the information provided and the consequences if the information is falsified should go at the end of the application. This type of statement, once developed for your organization, should be reviewed by a lawyer. For example:

Applicant's Documentation Verification and Agreement

I hereby confirm that the information provided on this application is true and complete to the best of my knowledge and authorize *(organization name)* to verify its accuracy and to obtain reference information on my work performance. I release *(organization name)* from any and all liability of whatever kind and nature that at any time could result from obtaining and having an employment decision based on such information.

I understand that, if employed, falsified statements of any kind or omissions of facts called for on this application shall be considered sufficient basis for dismissal.

I understand that should an employment offer be extended to me and accepted, I will fully adhere to all the policies, procedures, rules, and regulations of *(organization name)*. I also understand that anything said or implied during the interview process shall not constitute or imply an employment contract.

_____

Signature of applicant

Phone Interview Questions

Phone Interview Questions for Early Childhood Teacher Candidates

In our hiring profile, we want to look for individuals who have positive self-perceptions (seem to be can-do people) and, at the same time, identify well with people from diverse backgrounds. Here are some questions to ask that will help you gain insight into these characteristics:

1. Tell about a situation in which you were very successful. What happened, what did you do, and what was the outcome?

2. Tell about a situation in which you were involved with a person from a different ethnic, religious, or racial background.

3. What is it that allows you to be successful in working with people very different from you?

4. What personal accomplishments are you most proud of and why?

5. If you were guaranteed to accomplish at least one major task in your lifetime, what would that accomplishment be?

6. How would you handle the challenge of creating a common sense of purpose in an organization of highly diverse individuals?

Reprinted with permission from Northern Kentucky University's Early Childhood Center.

152

One-on-One Interview Questions

Interview Questions for Early Childhood Teacher Candidates to Determine Competence

1. What are some of the most exciting recent developments in early childhood?

2. Where do you see the next major developments taking place in early childhood?

3. If you had to identify an area of expertise within early childhood, what would yours be?

4. What things about early childhood do you find most exciting?

5. What do you see as the special challenges of early childhood in a program such as the NKU Early Childhood Center?

6. What kind of contribution do you anticipate making at the NKU Early Childhood Center?

7. What aspects of your work do you find most enjoyable or fulfilling?

8. What are the most important factors in establishing long-term working relationships with families, students, and colleagues?

9. What are the greatest challenges that face early childhood and higher education in the coming decade?

10. What do you see as early childhood's most important contribution to American society today? What about higher education?

Reprinted with permission from Northern Kentucky University's Early Childhood Center.

153

Working Interview Questions for Teacher Candidates

Parent Feedback Form

Use during teaching demonstration. Please use back for additional comments.

	Didn't observe		Some		Often
Approachable	1	2	3	4	5
Listens and responds	1	2	3	4	5
Interacts with me and my child in a way that shows interest in developing a partnership	1	2	3	4	5
Friendly and respectful	1	2	3	4	5
Interacts with me in a professional manner	1	2	3	4	5
Seems genuinely interested in creating an environment that will strengthen the development of my child	1	2	3	4	5
Other:	1	2	3	4	5

Staff Feedback Form

Use during teaching demonstration. Please use back for additional comments.

	Didn't observe	Some			Often
Friendly, warm, and affectionate	1	2	3	4	5
Bends low for child-level interaction	1	2	3	4	5
Encourages independence and self-help	1	2	3	4	5
Allows kids to problem solve, intervening if necessary	1	2	3	4	5
Reinforces positive behavior	1	2	3	4	5
Calm and relaxed manner in child interactions	1	2	3	4	5
Anticipates problems and redirects	1	2	3	4	5
Aware of developmental levels and plans age-appropriate skills	1	2	3	4	5
Practices, models, and maintains health and safety procedures	1	2	3	4	5
Maintains awareness of the whole group and the activity space, even while interacting individually with 1 child	1	2	3	4	5
Listens to other staff, asks questions, tries out suggestions	1	2	3	4	5
Activity aligns with program philosophy	1	2	3	4	5
Other:	1	2	3	4	5

Observer Feedback Form

Use during teaching demonstration. Please use back for additional comments.

	Didn't observe		Some		Often
Handles transitions well	1	2	3	4	5
Handles difficult situations well	1	2	3	4	5
Talks with individual children; provides language development opportunities	1	2	3	4	5
Encourages prosocial behavior in children such as cooperation, helping, taking turns, negotiating, problem solving	1	2	3	4	5
Responds to children's needs and interests	1	2	3	4	5
Interacts with children showing warmth and respect	1	2	3	4	5
Encourages children to clean up; participates in cleanup as needed; reinforces children's efforts	1	2	3	4	5
Other:	1	2	3	4	5

Staff Orientation Checklist

Name _____

Date of hire _____   First orientation date _____

Program Information Review

☐ employment application

☐ education documentation

☐ in-service hour

☐ program mission and vision

☐ organizational chart

☐ probationary period and salary

☐ job description

☐ program hours

☐ work schedule

☐ program phone numbers

☐ director's home and work phone numbers

☐ principal's phone number

☐ janitor's phone number

Policy and Procedures Review

☐ time sheet

☐ payroll

☐ benefits

☐ late/sick policy

☐ first aid kits
incident reports
calling 911

☐ children's files

☐ mobile phone usage
(personal and program phones)

☐ confidentiality

☐ staff expectations

☐ field trip responsibilities

☐ medical consent to treat

☐ child pickup and drop-off

☐ hand washing and food preparation
For those using USDA food reimbursements:
"What's in a Meal"

☐ payment schedule

☐ dress code

☐ lesson plan due dates

☐ blank lesson plan

☐ resource library

☐ ratios

☐ use of walkie-talkies

☐ mandatory reporting of child abuse

☐ staff meeting dates

☐ mandatory parent meetings and open
houses

☐ procedure for requesting classroom items

☐ emergency procedures

☐ fire

☐ sick child

☐ tornado

☐ inebriated parent

☐ unauthorized pickup

☐ shelter in place

☐ planning times

☐ behavior management philosophy

☐ training required

☐ first aid and CPR training:

    Date _____ Renewal _____

☐ child abuse training:

    Date _____ Renewal _____

☐ communicable disease training:

    Date _____ Renewal _____

☐ evaluation

☐ date scheduled for evaluation _____

☐ blank copy of evaluation form

☐ professional development plan

☐ date of next meeting (usually 1 month after hire) _____

_____   _____

Signature of supervisor   Date

_____   _____

Signature of employee   Date

Employee should receive the following documents:

- copy of this form
- family handbook
- staff handbook
- licensing rules
- NAEYC Code of Ethics

Please read the family and staff handbooks. If you have any questions, please see the director.

Topics for Staff and Family Handbooks

Staff Handbook

Introduction
- philosophy
- mission
- acronyms

Equal opportunity employer

Inclusion statement

Hours of operation

Organizational chart

Chain of command

Staff qualification

Job descriptions

Salary scale

Benefits
- disability insurance
- family and medical leave
- incentives
- jury duty
- life insurance
- medical, dental, and vision insurance
- retirement
- sick and personal days
- staff discount for child care
- unemployment compensation
- vacations and holidays
- workers' compensation

NAEYC Code of Ethics

Staff evaluations

Professional development requirements

Professional development plan and grievance procedures
- grounds for termination
- harassment policy
- policy and procedures
- privacy act (employee records)
- resignation
- staff conduct expectations
- staff mediation

Arrival and departure
- authorized and unauthorized pickup
- late pickup
- signing in and out

Computer use
- Internet access
- intranet access
- software modifications

Discipline policy (children's)

Drop-in policy

Lesson plan guidelines

Computers, tablets, and mobile phones
- issued
- lost
- mobile phone, tablet, or computer abuse
- return at the end of service
- use of personal mobile phone

Name badges issued and replacement cost

Photograph release (adult and child)

Room cleanup responsibilities

Sick day call-in procedures

Staff meetings

Staff orientation

Phone calls and messages

Television and film usage

Outdoor temperature

Travel guidelines

Safety practices
- accidents, reporting form
- minor
- serious
- calling 911
- supervision of outdoor activities

- adult pickup under the influence
- emergency drills
- shelter in place
- lockdown
- fire
- tornado
- earthquake
- emergency closings for electrical, plumbing, or other issues
- snow days
- hand-washing policy
- illness policy
- administering medication
- sunscreen
- cough drops
- nebulizers and inhalers, epinephrine (EpiPen), glucometer
- missing child policy
- reporting accidents and injuries
- safety checklists (indoors and outdoors)
- mandated reporter
- tobacco use policy
- unfamiliar person in center
- volunteers not in ratio

Ratio and group size

Field trips
- extra adults
- linked to learning
- lunches
- family consent
- family reminders
- preapproval
- transportation

Use of copier, printer, and laminator

Use of kitchen
Use of break room
Use of resource library
Breaks
Meals and snacks

Use of restrooms
• staff
• child
Dress code
Personal property storage
Birthday celebrations (children)

Teacher-owned versus school-owned materials
Classroom expenses
Outreach services
Community resources

Family Handbook

Table of contents
Philosophy
Mission
Goals
Hours of operation
Fee structure
• part-time and full-time options
• multiple-child discount
• sliding fee scale
• scholarships
• child care subsidy eligibility
• late pickup
• payment of fees
• returned check policy
Enrollment procedures
Immunization requirements
Special needs statement
Arrival and departure procedures
Orientation
Activities offered
Meals offered
• USDA, CACFP
• menus posted or sent in newsletter
• food allergies
Daily schedule
Program visitation
Volunteering
Two-week vacation option
Notifying the program of a sick child
• sick children (in program)
• isolation
• parent notification (child illness or accident)

• return to program after illness
• fever policy
• allergies
• notification of communicable diseases
Hand washing
Children with special needs
Reporting accidents and injuries
Mandated reporting of suspected child abuse
Field trips
Photo release
Technology
Communication
Under the influence
Transportation
• in the event of an accident or injury
• field trip
• to and from school
Emergencies
• drills (fire, tornado, lockdown)
• snow days
• loss of electricity, water, and so on
After-hours child care by staff
Lost and found
What to bring from home
• washing of napping items
• naptime
Storage of children's belongings
Discipline policy
Communicating with staff
• daily during drop-off and pickup

• scheduled in-person conference
• scheduled phone conference
• suggestion box
• notes
• completing periodic surveys
NAEYC Code of Ethics
• parents' rights
• children's rights
• confidentiality
Outreach services
Community resources
Transitioning children into program
Summer child care options

Sample Staff Evaluation

Job Performance Evaluation Form

(Your organization's name)

Decide on the terms you will use for the evaluation, and then define them. For instance, let's say you choose the following evaluation terms:

- Exceeds expectations
- Meets expectations
- Below expectations

Next, you have to define what each term means, as in the following example:

- Exceeds expectations: Employee routinely surpasses job responsibilities.
- Meets expectations: Employee is consistently proficient and reliable.
- Below expectations: Employee frequently fails to meet job responsibilities.

Using your job description, you will also need to decide what performance measures you will evaluate and then define them, as in the following example.

Administration: Organized, effectively manages the budget, prepares an effective marketing plan, maintains enrollment, maintains adult-child ratios and maximum groups sizes for each classroom.

☐ Exceeds expectations
☐ Meets expectations
☐ Below expectations
☐ NA

Training: Maintains the prescribed amount of training required by licensing, accreditation, and QRIS. Turns in paperwork to confirm attendance. Obtains all trainings listed on annual professional development plan.

☐ Exceeds expectations
☐ Meets expectations
☐ Below expectations
☐ NA

Lesson plans: Creates developmentally appropriate lesson plans, turns in plans on time, and posts plans on the family board and in the program space.

☐ Exceeds expectations
☐ Meets expectations
☐ Below expectations
☐ NA

Communication: Both oral and written communications are professional. Shares ideas and concerns and is an active partner in finding solutions. Communicates with families and coworkers about pertinent program information in a timely manner.

☐ Exceeds expectations
☐ Meets expectations
☐ Below expectations
☐ NA

Teamwork: Works effectively with coworkers and respects the rights of children, families, and staff. Maintains a cooperative work ethic, and seeks to work as participating team member.

☐ Exceeds expectations
☐ Meets expectations
☐ Below expectations
☐ NA

Decision making and problem solving: Uses the program's policy and procedures manual to solve problems and seeks out advice when unaware of proper decision. Addresses family concerns and problems professionally and promptly.

☐ Exceeds expectations
☐ Meets expectations
☐ Below expectations
☐ NA

Expense management: Spends the classroom supply budget responsibly and turns in receipts for materials purchased. When accessing petty cash, fills out the petty cash slips and attaches receipts.

Administration only: Generates a programwide budget and reviews it monthly. Reallocates funds appropriately.

☐ Exceeds expectations
☐ Meets expectations
☐ Below expectations
☐ NA

Classroom and program management: Maintains a developmentally appropriate classroom with age-appropriate activities, materials, and supplies. Creates a behavior management plan that allows children to internalize their own behavior and teaches children how to cope in stressful situations. Creates a family-friendly and respectful environment for all children and their families.

Administration only: Selects qualified people effectively. Conducts unbiased evaluations yearly, outlining staff strengths and weaknesses while providing supportive and constructive feedback. Works with individual employees to create professional development plans.

☐ Exceeds expectations
☐ Meets expectations
☐ Below expectations
☐ NA

Paperwork: Turns in time sheets, daily attendance, lesson plans, and activity materials at the predetermined time.

☐ Exceeds expectations
☐ Meets expectations
☐ Below expectations
☐ NA

Job knowledge: Uses developmentally appropriate strategies to create an environment and lesson plans that are responsive to the needs of the children enrolled. Utilizes individualized lesson plans and creates activities and spaces that are intentionally designed for a specific purpose and skill development. Shares these strategies with the families of the children they serve.

☐ Exceeds expectations
☐ Meets expectations
☐ Below expectations
☐ NA

Leadership: Takes the lead and is willing to mentor other staff when approached. Works effectively with others, and takes leadership roles in activities and events.

☐ Exceeds expectations
☐ Meets expectations
☐ Below expectations
☐ NA

Program improvement and agent of change: Works continually to improve the program and is an active partner in accreditation and QRIS processes. Works to review policy and procedures outlined in the family and staff handbooks and positively engages in the process of change.

☐ Exceeds expectations
☐ Meets expectations
☐ Below expectations
☐ NA

Customer friendliness: Is responsive to children, families, and coworkers. Greets others with respect and attention. Responds to questions and concerns in a timely manner.

☐ Exceeds expectations
☐ Meets expectations
☐ Below expectations
☐ NA

Dependability: Is on time for work and is available when asked. Completes tasks in a timely manner.

☐ Exceeds expectations
☐ Meets expectations
☐ Below expectations
☐ NA

Safety: Conducts a weekly inside safety check and daily outside safety check. Reports needs for repairs promptly. Keeps dangerous materials out of the reach of children at all times. Makes sure adequate supervision is in place when conducting field trips and when activities need small groups in order to be safe.

☐ Exceeds expectations
☐ Meets expectations
☐ Below expectations
☐ NA

Attire: Maintains a clean appearance. Does not wear tank tops or clothing with inappropriate words or holes. Wears closed-toed shoes at all times.

☐ Exceeds expectations
☐ Meets expectations
☐ Below expectations
☐ NA

Once you have created your staff performance evaluation form, rate each individual in each of the performance measures. Give three points for "exceeds expectations," two points for "meets expectations," and one point for "below expectations." Points allow you to quantify the evaluation. When giving a staff member "exceeds" or "does not meet," examples should be included to substantiate the rating.

Areas of Strength and Successes

In this section, list the employee's areas of strength, accomplishments, and successful project work that relate directly to the employee's job responsibilities, as well as social interactions that you appreciate. In addition, list positive comments made by families and coworkers.

Areas for Improvement

In this section, list the employee's areas for improvement with examples of why improvement is needed.

Professional Development Plan (Plan for Continuing Growth)

In this section, create a professional development plan based on your evaluation that outlines training, personal growth expectations, and job expectations that have not been met, as well as a plan to meet these expectations.

Employee Comments

This section allows the employee to make comments about the evaluation, such as objecting to the overall review or to certain portions. The employee can also note here appreciation for an unbiased, well-rounded evaluation process.

Signatures

_____   _____

Evaluated by   Date

_____   _____

Reviewed with employee by   Date

_____   _____

Employee   Date

(Employee signature does not necessarily indicate agreement with the evaluation; it means that the employee was given an opportunity to discuss the evaluation with the supervisor.)

Sample Job Performance Warning

Job Performance Warning

Date _____

Name of employee _____

Job title _____   **Date of hire** _____

Type of warning

☐ verbal (counseling)   ☐ written   ☐ dismissal

Policy or Procedure Violation

Describe in detail what policy or procedure was violated, who was present, and whom you interviewed during the investigation prior to issuing this warning.

Actions Taken

Outline the actions that will be taken. These could include counseling, a day off without pay, a plan of action that will help the employee meet or exceed the job expectation violated, and so on.

Staff Comments

The employee may comment about the warning or the process here.

Signatures

_____   _____
Reviewed with employee by   Date

_____   _____
Employee   Date

(Employee signature does not necessarily indicate agreement with the warning; it means that the employee was given an opportunity to discuss this action with the supervisor.)

Sample Payroll Deduction Authorization Form

(Your organization's name)

(Your organization's address)

I hereby authorize *(your organization's name)* to deduct the following amounts from my gross pay each pay period. If the deduction amount changes within the fiscal year, *(your organization's name)* is authorized to deduct the new amount from my pay.

If a new payroll deduction authorization form is not submitted to management on or before the start of the next fiscal year, this form shall be deemed to continue in force for the next fiscal year.

Payroll deductions

Retirement	$ _____
Health insurance	$ _____
Vision insurance	$ _____
Dental insurance	$ _____
Long- and short-term disability	$ _____
Life insurance	$ _____
Child support	$ _____
Child care	$ _____
Union dues	$ _____
Wage garnishment	$ _____
Other	$ _____

_____   _____

Employee signature   Date

Resources

Bennis, Warren, and Joan Goldsmith. 2010. *Learning to Lead: A Workbook on Becoming a Leader*. 4th ed. New York: Basic Books.

Bergen, Sharon. 2016. *Early Childhood Staff Orientation Guide*. Saint Paul, MN: Redleaf Press.

Blanchard, Ken, and Spencer Johnson. 2015. *The New One Minute Manager*. New York: William Morrow.

Borman Fink, Dale. 2006. *Doing the Right Thing: Ethical Development across Diverse Environments*. San Francisco: Jossey-Bass/Wiley.

Copeland, Tom. 2012. *Family Child Care Marketing Guide*. 2nd ed. Saint Paul, MN: Redleaf Press.

DePree, Max. 2004. *Leadership Is an Art*. New York: Doubleday.

Jorde Bloom, Paula. 1982. *Avoiding Burnout: Strategies for Managing Time, Space, and People in Early Childhood Education*. Lake Forest, IL: New Horizons.

Loflin, Jones, and Todd Musig. 2007. *Juggling Elephants: An Easier Way to Get Your Most Important Things Done—Now!* New York: Penguin Books.

Lundin, Stephen C., Harry Paul, and John Christensen. 2002. *Fish! Tales: The #1 Way to Boost Morale*. New York: Hyperion.

Maggio, Rosalie. 2009. *How to Say It: Choice Words, Phrases, Sentences, and Paragraphs for Every Situation*. 3rd ed. New York: Prentice Hall.

Miller, Brian Cole. 2004. *Quick Team-Building Activities for Busy Managers*. New York: AMACOM.

Morgenstern, Julie. 2004. *Time Management from the Inside Out: The Foolproof System for Taking Control of Your Schedule—and Your Life*. 2nd ed. New York: Henry Holt.

Nash, Robert J. 2002. *"Real World" Ethics: Frameworks for Educators and Human Service Professionals*. 2nd ed. New York: Teachers College Press.

Nelson, Bob. 2012. *1,501 Ways to Reward Employees*. New York: Workman Publishing.

Newman, Roberta L. 2002. *Training New After-School Staff: Welcome to the World of School-Age Care!* Nashville: School-Age NOTES.

Nichols, Michael P. 2009. *The Lost Art of Listening: How Learning to Listen Can Improve Relationships*. 2nd ed. New York: Guilford Press.

Sciarra, Dorothy June, and Anne G. Dorsey. 2002. *Leaders and Supervisors in Child Care Programs*. Clifton Park, NY: Delmar.

Seiler, William J., Melissa L. Beall, and Joseph P. Mazer. 2016. *Communication: Making Connections*. 10th ed. New York: Pearson.

Seligson, Michelle, and Patricia Stahl. 2003. *Bringing Yourself to Work: A Guide to Successful Staff Development in After-School Programs*. New York: Teachers College Press.

Stone, Douglas, Bruce Patton, and Sheila Heen. 2010. *Difficult Conversations: How to Discuss What Matters Most*. 10th-anniversary ed. New York: Penguin Books.

Venolia, Carol. 1995. *Healing Environments*. Berkeley, CA: Celestial Arts.

References

American Marketing Association (AMA). 2013. "Definition of Marketing." www.ama
.org/AboutAMA/Pages/Definition-of-Marketing.aspx.

Bennis, Warren, and Patricia Ward Biederman. 1997. *Organizing Genius: The Secrets of Creative Collaboration*. Reading, MA: Addison-Wesley.

Biden, Joe. 2008. "In Their Own Words: Senator Joe Biden." www.pjvoice.com/v39
/39303biden.aspx.

Blanchard Ken, and Don Hutson. 2008. *The One Minute Entrepreneur*. New York: Doubleday.

Blanchard, Ken, and Spencer Johnson. 2015. *The New One Minute Manager*. New York: William Morrow.

Bryant, Andy, and Charlie Mawer. 2016. *The TV Brand Builders: How to Win Audiences and Influence Viewers*. Philadelphia: Kogan Page Publishers.

Carnegie, Andrew. 1999. "American Experience: Andrew Carnegie." www.pbs.org
/wgbh/amex/carnegie/peopleevents/pande01.html.

Churchill, Winston. 1952. "Debate on the Address." www.nationalchurchillmuseum
.org/blog/category/winston-churchill-quotes/.

Covey, Steven M. R. 2006. *The Speed of Trust: The One Thing That Changes Everything*. New York: Free Press.

Cutler, Thomas J., ed. 2015. *The U.S. Naval Institute on Naval Leadership*. Annapolis, MD: Naval Institute Press.

DePree, Max. 2004. *Leadership Is an Art*. New York: Doubleday.

Drucker, Peter F. 1986. *Management: Tasks, Responsibilities, Practices*. New York: Truman Talley Books.

Fisk, Carlton. 2000. "Carlton Fisk's Hall of Fame Induction Speech." www.redsox
diehard.com/players/fiskspeech.html.

Gallagher, Taffy. 2009. *100 Ideas to Market Your Childcare Business*. Bloomington, IN: iUniverse.

Grossman, Shelia, and Theresa Valiga. 2013. *The New Leadership Challenge: Creating the Future of Nursing*. 4th ed. Philadelphia: F. A. Davis Company.

Havel, Vaclav. 1990. *Disturbing the Peace*. New York: Vintage Books.

Hickman, Craig R., and Michael A. Silva. 1987. *The Future 500: Creating Tomorrow's Organizations Today*. New York: New American Library.

Iacocca, Lee. 2007. *Iacocca: An Autobiography*. New York: Bantam Dell.

ICF International. 2016. "National Child Care Information Center (NCCIC)."
www.icfi.com/insights/projects/families-and-communities/national-child-care
-information-center.

Jantsch, John. 2006. *Duct Tape Marketing: The World's Most Practical Small Business Marketing Guide*. Nashville, TN: Thomas Nelson.

Knowles, Elizabeth, ed. 2007. *Oxford Dictionary of Modern Quotations*. New York: Oxford University Press.

Lindsay, Larry M., and Mark A. Smith. 2007. *Leading Change in Your World*. 3rd ed. Marion, IN: Triangle Publishing.

Loflin, Jones, and Todd Musig. 2007. *Juggling Elephants: An Easier Way to Get Your Most Important Things Done—Now!* New York: Penguin Books.

Lundin, Stephen C. 2002. *Fish! Tales: Real-Life Stories to Help You Transform Your Workplace and Your Life.* New York: ChartHouse Learning.

Mayo Clinic. 2015. "Work-Life Balance: Tips to Reclaim Control." www.mayoclinic.org/healthy-lifestyle/adult-health/in-depth/work-life-balance/art-20048134.

Miller, Henry. 1941. *The Wisdom of the Heart.* New York: New Directions Books.

Miner, Margaret, and Hugh Rawson, eds. 2006. *The Oxford Dictionary of American Quotations.* New York: Oxford University Press.

Morita, Akio. 1984. *Made in Japan: Akio Morita and Sony.* New York: E. P. Dutton.

Nelson, Bob. 2012. *1,501 Ways to Reward Employees.* New York: Workman Publishing.

Nichols, Michael P. 2009. *The Lost Art of Listening: How Learning to Listen Can Improve Relationships.* 2nd ed. New York: Guilford Press.

Office of Child Care (OCC). 2016. "Office of Child Care." www.acf.hhs.gov/programs/occ.

Podmoroff, Dianna. 2005. *365 Ways to Motivate and Reward Your Employees Every Day—with Little or No Money.* Ocala, FL: Atlantic Publishing Group.

Powell, Colin. 2001. *A Soldier's Way: An Autobiography.* London: Arrow Books.

Reagan, Ronald. 1986. "Reagan on Decision-Making, Planning, Gorbachev, and More." *Fortune.* September 15.

Rouse, Margaret. 2016. "Definition: Meta Tag." http://searchsoa.techtarget.com/definition/meta-tag.

Sciarra, Dorothy June, and Anne G. Dorsey. 2002. *Leaders and Supervisors in Child Care Programs.* Clifton Park, NY: Delmar.

Surowiecki, James. 2014. "The Cult of Overwork." www.newyorker.com/magazine/2014/01/27/the-cult-of-overwork.

Talan, Teri N., and Paula Jorde Bloom. 2009. *Business Administration Scale for Family Child Care.* New York: Teachers College Press.

———. 2011. *Program Administration Scale: Measuring Early Childhood Leadership and Management.* 2nd ed. New York: Teachers College Press.

US Department of Agriculture (USDA). 2015. "Child and Adult Care Food Program." www.fns.usda.gov/cacfp.

US Department of Health and Human Services. 2016. "Office of Child Care." www.acf.hhs.gov/programs/occ.

US Department of Justice Civil Rights Division. 2016. "Information and Technical Assistance on the Americans with Disabilities Act." www.ada.gov.

US Department of Labor (DOL). 2009. "Fact Sheet #46: Daycare Centers and Preschools Under the Fair Labor Standards Act (FLSA)." www.dol.gov/whd/regs/compliance/whdfs46.pdf.

———. 2016. "Occupational Safety and Health Administration." www.osha.gov.

US Equal Employment Opportunity Center. 2016. "Prohibited Employment Policies/Practices." www.eeoc.gov/laws/practices/.

US Small Business Administration (SBA). 2015. "How to Fire an Employee and Stay within the Law." www.sba.gov/blogs/how-fire-employee-and-stay-within-law.

Index